To Daddy

With lots of love

Patty O'Sullivan

29-09-2011

GROWING UP ON THE CURRAGH

Memories of Childhood in the Curragh Military Camp before and during the Second World War

Patricia O'Sullivan

ORIGINAL WRITING

© 2011 Patricia O'Sullivan

All rights reserved. No part of this publication may be reproduced in any form or by any means—graphic, electronic or mechanical, including photocopying, recording, taping or information storage and retrieval systems—without the prior written permission of the author.

ISBN: 978-1-908024-24-4

A CIP catalogue for this book is available from the National Library.

Published by ORIGINAL WRITING LTD., Dublin, 2011.

Printed in Great Britain by MPG BOOKS GROUP,
Bodmin and Kings Lynn

Dedication

I dedicate this memoir to my parents, John and Annie O'Sullivan, and in particular my mother, Annie, who devoted her life to rearing her ten children with love and encouragement in everything they attempted. "Thank you Mammy, you were taken from us far too soon, but we have always known you were there guiding us." My thanks also to my siblings who are still with us, Emmet, Dermot, Bernie, Irene, Emer, and Donal. They contradicted my memory on occasion, although they knew they were 'talking to the wall'!

I should also like to include in this dedication all those who spent their childhood in that very special place, the Curragh. If you read this memoir, I hope you will enjoy it.

Lives of Great Men all remind us

We can make our lives sublime

And departing, leave behind us

Footprints on the sands of time

A Psalm of Life

Henry Wadsworth Longfellow 1807

Introduction

In conversations with my contemporaries we often compare the way life is now, and how it was when we were young growing up. Many of us were born in the thirties, or even earlier. Then, throughout the world, the constant struggle to survive during those years of economic depression was the norm for most families.

Ireland was no exception. In fact, Ireland was in a much more difficult situation economically than most countries. Not only had we the fallout from the Great War, we were still suffering the aftermath of the Civil War. Unemployment was rife, social welfare barely minimum, and emigration had become a way of life.

In discussing our individual childhoods, I was, however, surprised to learn that, unlike my family, some of my contemporaries had grown up without the facilities of running water, electricity, and also without good access to health care. Several had to leave school at 14, in order to work to help with the financial demands of their families. Secondary education was not free, and for many families, was unaffordable, especially as the average family in those days consisted of more than eight children.

There was, of course, the County Council Scholarship, eligibility for which was strictly means tested. Besides, in some counties only three scholarships were awarded, so competition was great in order to win this very hard fought examination. It is a credit to the children brought up in this era, and to the teaching in the primary schools at that time, that most, irrespective of their educational backgrounds, went on to lead successful and fulfilling lives.

The reason why my own childhood was relatively different, was not because I came from a 'privileged' or rich background, but simply because I was born and spent my childhood on the Curragh. To be precise, I was fortunate to have been born in the Curragh Military Camp, where we lived, not by any means in luxury, but we did have the benefits of running water, electricity, good schools and very good health care, as well as great sports facilities.

In those days living in the Camp, surrounded on all four sides by the wide Curragh Plains, made us feel as though we were living on our own little island. I suppose for this reason I sometimes find it difficult to enter fully into discussions with my contemporaries regarding our childhoods. In order to capture, in some small way, a childhood in a different time and in a unique place that is no more, I have written this memoir.

Contents

Introduction — iv

Prologue — ix

Part 1

Chapter One
THE CURRAGH — 1

Chapter Two
EARLIEST MEMORIES — 12

Chapter Three
EARLY YEARS — 14

Chapter Four
EARLY SCHOOLDAYS — 21

Chapter Five
FAMILY LIFE IN THE THIRTIES ON THE CURRAGH — 26

Chapter Six
THE ARMY AND US — 32

Chapter Seven
ENTERTAINMENT BEFORE THE WAR — 34

Chapter Eight
SPORTS, AND THE END OF AN ERA — 37

Part II

Chapter Nine
THE EMERGENCY AND EVACUATION — 45

Chapter Ten
SECONDARY SCHOOL — 50

Chapter Eleven
OUR NEW DOMAIN — 55

Chapter Twelve
FAMILY LIFE DURING THE EMERGENCY — 61

Chapter Thirteen
FOREIGNERS AMONG US — 68

Chapter Fourteen
SWIMMING AND OTHER SPORTS — 73

Chapter Fifteen
BIRTH AND CHANGES — 76

Chapter Sixteen
1945 — 81

Chapter Seventeen
END OF SCHOOLDAYS AND FACING THE FUTURE — 86

Epilogue — 91

Prologue

My father was born near Dromahane, in County Cork. In 1911 aged 17, after a row with his parents, he joined the British army. He enlisted in Mullingar, and was sent on a course to Longford, and subsequently to Aldershot in England, where he joined the Army Transport Corps. He fought throughout the Great War, was wounded in the Retreat from Mons, and was awarded several medals.

There is no agreement on the total number of Irish soldiers who served in the British Army and Navy in WW1, but some historians claim over 200,000. What is certain is that more than 49,000 lost their lives, and nearly every family in Ireland felt the loss of a family member or friend in that terrible carnage. Two of my father's brothers were killed.

In April 1922 my father took his discharge from the British Army, and in June returned to Ireland. What he didn't know of course, was that Ireland was in the throes of a civil war, the Pro-Treaty forces—the Free-Staters, fighting the Anti-Treaty forces—the Republicans. This was surely not the welcome the war weary soldier expected!

He described how, walking down what is now Pearse Street, he encountered some Free State soldiers arguing about how to work a very large artillery piece, the workings of which they seemed to have no idea. My father, familiar with the piece from his years in the British army and 4 years of war, was able to show them how to work the weaponry.

As the authorities became aware of his engineering experience and his excellent discharge papers and, of course, his medals, he was encouraged to join the Free State Army. As he said himself, that was the beginning of his life in the Irish Army. Later in the late twenties early thirties, he joined the newly formed Irish Defence Forces or Oglaigh na hEireann. Thus, began his army career of over 34 years, most of which was spent in the Curragh Camp, Co. Kildare

He had met my mother in Mullingar in 1923, and in September of that year they were married in St. Joseph's Church in Boyle, Co. Roscommon. . After his marriage they lived in Dublin where my brother Harold was born on 31st August 1924. A year later they moved to the Curragh, where their family grew and grew in size. As an appreciation of their life together and of their many sacrifices, I have written this memoir of my childhood until I was 18. It will, I hope, give a picture of what it was like growing up as one of an extending family, in a military establishment in Ireland, during the thirties and forties.

Part 1

Chapter One

THE CURRAGH

I feel sure that today, most people will have an idea of what the Curragh Plains look like, particularly if they are driving between Newbridge and Kildare, or out for a day at the Curragh Races. It presents a beautiful tableau, wide green plains, dotted with furze bushes, whose bright yellow flowers bloomed for several months of the year. In the distance the ever-changing colour of the Wicklow Mountains stand as a back drop to the picture. In the early morning, one can see the most beautiful racehorses galloping across the plains in their early morning rides. And of course, there are, the ubiquitous sheep—the enduring inhabitants of the Curragh Plains.

But smack in the middle we see something strange—are those woods? Is that a castle in the woods, with its flag flying proudly? If we look closer we can see a very tall Clock Tower—in the middle of the woods?

No, what we are looking at is the Curragh Military Camp, hidden on three sides by plantations of tall green trees. That is not a castle, but the Water Tower, and yes, that is a Clock Tower. Both buildings were erected more than a hundred years ago—the Clock Tower almost 150, and whose upper galleries were used in its early years as a watchtower for the British military surveying the adjacent countryside. The woods now surrounding the camp were mere saplings when I was a child, and some had yet to be been planted. In those days they were known as the plantations—a wonderful place for us to play cowboys and Indians.

Those of us who lived in the Curragh then rarely referred to it as the Curragh Camp—it was always The Curragh. A camp for us was something we built in the trenches surrounding the Camp, with old blankets, galvanized iron and wooden sticks –but more about that later.

The Curragh Camp as a military establishment was built by the British in the middle of the 19th Century, at the time of the Crimean War. It expanded rapidly, and between 1894 and 1910 the place as I knew it in the 1930s and forties, was complete. After our Treaty with Britain of 1922, it was 'handed over to the Irish Army'. When we were young, we loved to listen to this description, feeling the excitement felt by the Free State Army, when in 1922, they marched into the Curragh Camp, "whilst passing the British Army on the way out".

I hope the following description will give the reader an insight into this place where ten of us grew up and the history into which we were born.

The British built some very fine buildings. Some of our favourites growing up were the aforementioned Water Tower/Fire Station, the Post Office, the Clock Tower, the two Churches, the Military Hospital, and the School. Besides these very imposing buildings the Curragh housed seven military barracks, each with living accommodation for the troops, and separate housing for families.

The individual barracks were named after the seven signatories of the 1916 Declaration, Plunkett, Ceannt, Connolly, Clarke, McDermott, McDonagh, and Pearse. The living accommodation for the families, was mostly two and three bed room terraced houses, and as with the majority of the buildings in the camp, were built of red brick. All the houses had running water, electricity and a weekly a supply of coal. When I was born we lived in McDermot Terrace.

Growing up in the houses in the individual barracks, one developed an almost tribal allegiance to the one in which we lived. They were like seven little enclaves or tiny villages, but all were

PATRICIA O'SULLIVAN

My Parents, John & Annie with brother Harold   c. 1925

My father's arrival in the Curragh c.1925

GROWING UP ON THE CURRAGH

Harold and Sean, Dublin c.1927

Harold and Sean, Dublin. c. 1929

PATRICIA O'SULLIVAN

*Fire Station, Father driver,
c. 1933*

Outside Fire Station c. 1932

GROWING UP ON THE CURRAGH

Harold, Patty and Sean

Patty, early 1932
Note soft ball in left hand

Brownstown Cross . c. 1932

Celebrating Eucharistic Congress 1932. Our family left on top and Neighbours, Murtaghs and possibly Brownes

Early 30's Note PA controlling traffic from Newbridge etc.

GROWING UP ON THE CURRAGH

My First Holy Communion – c. 1934

Family Photo taken behind the Fire Station by my father. 1935 from left our dog Bunch, Paddy Sheridan, Harold, Joan, Dermot Patty, Emmet, Sean, Vinnie Sheridan, Hughie Gallagher and 'Sullivan' from the bakery

PATRICIA O'SULLIVAN

The Monaghan Family 1939

*Mammy and her 5 daughters 1941.
From left Joan, Mammy with baby Emer in Arms, Patty,
in front, Bernie and Irene.*

GROWING UP ON THE CURRAGH

Harold with towel in this hand second from left 1941.

'The Chocolate Soldiers' Harold 2nd row
from top, third from right 1941.
A well washed uniform!

very proud to be part of the Curragh. However, in this respect to the outside world, all the inhabitants showed a fierce solidarity.

The landmark approach to the Camp from the north was of course the mighty Water Tower. It stands six hundred feet high, and this fine vantage point gave us a superb panorama of the surrounding countryside, with the Camp itself mapped out below like a Garden City. Part of my father's job at the Fire Station entailed the lowering of the flag on the roof every evening, and occasionally, as a special treat he would take us with him to the top to admire the view.

The roads leading out of the Curragh went north towards Newbridge, south to Brownstown, east towards Athgarvan and Kilcullen, and west to Kildare. The road north to south bisected the camp and it is here I'll begin my description of the place in which we lived.

Approaching the main entry to the Curragh Camp from the north, apart from seeing the Water Tower and Clock Tower, one noticed the absence of any large gates. This might have seemed surprising considering we were now entering a large and important military camp. However, as the road neared the camp proper, a sentry box with a military policeman, known as a PA, stood guard, (on all four roads entering the camp, a sentry stood guard). His duty was to monitor movements, mainly motor vehicle, in and out of the camp.

Once past the sentry box, we entered the centre of the camp—something like the Main Street in a town, and always a centre of bustling activity. For us children it was a place of great excitement. On our right, towering above us was the Water Tower, on our left the Catholic Church, and to the side of this, the Clock Tower, surrounded by its water tanks. Further down to the left was the very large Post Office building, a beautiful brick building, occupying the corner where 4 roads meet.

Opposite the Water Tower and further down to the right was our particular pride and joy. This was Todd Burns, one of the most popular, and the largest shop on the Curragh. In today's world, one might call it a shopping centre. There were five departments within the complex, and also living quarters for the staff.

We knew all the sales staff, who seemed to remain the same, year in, and year out. The drapery department had specialist sections. One of these was the Man's Shop, presided over by Mr. Breslin. Sometimes he helped on the 'materials' counter in the fabric section. My mother would occasionally warn him to be careful about not cutting his fingers!!! Miss Purcell ran the Ladies and Children sections, as well as the haberdashery. She later left and opened her own shop next to O'Donnell's Grocery, near the market square.

Todd Burns's grocery was next door to the drapery, and to me was big, dark, and gloomy and not very enticing perhaps that is why we never bought sweets there. Next-door were the staff living quarters. The last building in the complex housed, on the right, a very big and modern Pharmacy, and on the left a China Shop. As a child the lovely coloured bottles scattered round the large bay windows in the chemist shop entranced me. The china shop was always very well stocked, with many beautiful tea sets, vases, and wine glasses of every description, as well as other house wares.

I should explain that although situated in a large military establishment in the true sense of the word, Todd Burns at that time was a thriving shopping centre and was possibly established during the British occupation of the Curragh. In today's world one could describe it as the Grafton Street of the Curragh Camp. The reader will probably laugh at this description, but remember this was the early thirties, and I can confidently say there was no other shop in the county outside the big cities, as big and, as I look back after eight decades, it was a very exciting place. We had our own little domain around this area, and were very happy children, and I can safely say that all of our friends felt the same.

To us the Curragh was a 'town' and the shops were terrific, particularly at Christmas. The toys appeared in Todd Burns's window mid-December, when the large windows were decorated for Christmas. Word went round at once, and so the competition to see who would be the first to reach the toys' windows began. We gazed longingly through the windows, each of us picking out what we wanted from Daddy Christmas. In those days, what we wanted and what we got was often wide off the mark!

Mr. Clune was the Manager. He, his wife, and two girls lived in a house at the end of the complex. The house separated Todd Burns from Farrell's shop, which was opposite the Post Office.

This was also a large shop, and at that time consisted of a garage, a car maintenance shop, newsagent and tobacconist, as well as a large sweet and confectionary section. My mother loved the newspapers, so we were sent up every evening to Farrells to get the Evening Herald, which would arrive on the 6pm bus. .

Eason's, surprised yes, we did have an Eason's, and I feel sure most people would be acquainted with the name, 'EASON'. It was a small shop but it had a lovely 'bookish' smell, and they allowed us children to look through the shelves. Of course the staff kept a watchful eye on us at the same time, just in case we slipped a comic up our jumpers! The shop was a wooden structure, painted red and the name, EASON was emblazoned in large print on the gable end.

We spent most of our pocket money (such as it was) in Eason's, buying penny or tuppeny comics. If we managed to save some pennies we could buy the Beano, the Dandy, Film Fun, or Radio Fun. But the favourite for the boys was the Hotspur. As we got older we learnt how to exchange our comics, and eventually we girls moved on to the Girls Crystal.

Eason's could be seen as far as the 'Church Bell,' from which we could swing when we grew tall enough and could climb the steep steps. Sometimes when we swung from the rope the bell would chime loudly. When this happened, we ran as if the whole army was after us—this added fear made the whole thing more exciting—it felt great, but nobody ever chased us.

There were, of course, many more shops other than Todd Burns, but it was the largest.

Further down this road on the other side, on the part we called the Dairy Hill; was Sheehan's, the shoemakers—Mick and Paddy, who spoke to us in Irish. They were very patriotic. Nextdoor were McAteers, the barbers, besides being a barber, Mr. McAteer bred Irish terriers, while Mrs. McAteer had a sweet shop. Their children Laurie and Joan were great swimmers.

At that time our next shop adjacent to McAteers, was our most favourite shop of all, 'Dairy Dobbyns'. There were two sisters (although I do believe there were three at this time). This was really our shop, with an array of lucky bags, sweets, ice creams etc. etc. They took no nonsense from us, but we liked them very much, and my mother always spoke very highly of them. At this time I think they also had a small teashop.

You see, as we lived across the road in McDermott Terrace, on the opposite side of the Dairy Hill, it was most convenient (probably too convenient, as my mother would say) to run across the road. We got 5 sweets for a halfpenny and 10 for a penny. We could also get 2 fizz bags for a penny, from which we might be fortunate to get a lucky dip as well.

At the bottom of the Dairy Hill was a crossroads, where the Dairy Hill bisected the Bottom Road. On the corner of the

Bottom Road on the left was a small block of shops. There was O'Donnell's grocery, and next door a drapery shop (later purchased by Miss Purcell after leaving Todd Burns), and a Man's shop. The latter I remember very well, because it had a little toy man in evening dress in the corner of the window that moved its head up and down. We used to spend some time imitating his actions, until we got bored. There was also living accommodation on this block which was occupied by a family called the Thornton's.

Diagonally across from this block of shops, was probably the most frequented building in the Camp. This was the Picture House—but more about that later.

We had a market square near here, further east along the Bottom Road. The market opened on Fridays, and was particularly popular for its fish, supplied by McCormack's from Newbridge. Sometimes there would be a vegetable stall, and of course, a second-hand clothes stall. There were two butchers shop, Conlon's and Orford's.

Also in this area was Crosses' Jewellry Shop, which was owned by a German Jew from Dublin, who was very short in stature and spoke much accented English. He regularly chased away the cheeky children, who crowded around his shop window, teasing him and imitating his accent. A constant refrain—repeated endlessly by the cheeky ones was, *"if vou vant to buy a vatch, buy a vatch, and don't be vatching all the vetches in my vindow!"* His shop only opened on a Wednesday—I expect that was as much as he could tolerate from the cheeky ones!

The square was quite large, and it was here that a most important annual event for us children took place. This was the arrival of Duffy's Circus and sometimes Fossett's Circus. The excitement we felt seeing the tent go up, and coming so close to the elephant that generally ignored us, was truly great.

Getting the entrance money was always a hassle—there were so many of us needing tickets—but my mother always came through with the money. I suppose it was a mixture of moral blackmail—long faces, ("everybody else is going"), and being on our best behaviour for days before the arrival of the circus. Many of the boys, including my brothers and their friends, always knew which part of the tent they could sneak under without paying. Of course, if they were caught they got a good hiding, occasionally even from the clowns!

Away from the market place and back up the Dairy Hill to the Water Tower, we continue our journey on the this road. Opposite Todd Burns was the Clock Tower which was adjacent to the Church grounds. The Church was a big wooden green structure with three alters. The choir was curtained off at the Sacred Heart side. The 'Stations of the Cross' were very impressive, and now adorn the walls of the new—(now 55 years old!) church.

There were four confessionals and four army chaplains, Frs. Carey, Prendergast, Fanning and Fitzsimons, and each had the rank of captain. We had our own favourite priest when going to confession. When I made my first confession I wanted to get out fast. It was dark, but the priest recognized me, and said, 'well Patty are you excited about the great day? He put me at ease immediately, but like most children at that time, I have never forgotten the trauma of my first confession.

After Mass on Sundays, we would wait for the priest who said Mass so that we could carry his prayer book to the Priest's House (it was a great honour to be handed this). I remember particularly Fr. Prendergast as he asked me what name my mother had called my new sister. I told him 'Irene' and he immediately said, a Greek word meaning 'Peace' He had many quotations. I was christened, made my First Communion and Confirmation in the church (St. Brigid's), as did most of my siblings.

Going down from the Church we come to our lovely post office, a large and very beautiful building. It stood proudly on the corner at the crossroad, occupying the whole corner spaces in both roads. I have to say we really loved looking at this building, and were very proud of it and whilst waiting for the Kildare bus on our way to Secondary School; we would run our hands over the stone work, particularly where the shine was. When we were tall enough to reach the broad windowsills on which we sat, we realized how many others must have sat there before us to give the sills their shiny surface.

Now we turn left at the crossroad going eastward, which brings us to a chemist shop, (I think it was called 'Dawson's' or 'Medical Hall'). This was also a very colourful shop with its shiny bottles. I think they had a branch in Newbridge as well. Donnelly Swift, the photographer was next door.

Donnelly Swift was a Curragh institution. As well as being the local and only photographer, he also ran the taxi service and car hire service. All our special occasion photos, as well as the important photographs of every other inhabitant of the Curragh, were taken in his studio. Many of these are included in the various pages of this memoir.

Continuing on, we pass Darlings barber and hairdressing shop, which was opened in the early 1900s during the time of the British. I am almost certain it was a small shop then, but was later rebuilt. Opposite Darlings we had the Catholic Soldiers' Home, where soldiers dropped in for a cup of tea and recreational activities. Continuing along this road, I think it was called McSweeney Road but we always called it the Middle Road, on the left were the two barracks, McDonagh and Pearse, with their married quarters on the other side of the road. With the Declaration of War in 1939 we would eventually get to know Pearse very well, and would spend the war years there, with a great spirit of adventure in all we did.

Coming back westwards towards the Post Office, on the left side of the road, we pass the Gaelic Hall (my first school). A little further along we come to the Protestant Church. This was a fine redbrick building standing on the corner opposite the post office. When we were children, very curious to know what was different about the church, we often sneaked in there to look around.

At the back of the church we had Lewis' Soldiers' Home. This was built on another road, set at a tangent to the main road and which led to the Gym. Lewis Soldiers Home catered for both soldiers and civilians, and was quite large. I think the building was officially called the Wesleyan Home, but we always called it Lewis. The Lewis family lived beside the café and my brothers played with their boys, and I sometimes tagged along (looking back now there seemed to be a shortage of girls of my own age at that time). The boys mostly played cowboys and Indians among the trees leading down to the Gym. My mother and Mrs. Lewis were good friends.

Crossing the central road going west from the Wesleyan Church you passed the remaining Barracks, at that time housing, I suppose about four Battalions, McDermot, Clarke, Ceannt (HQ) Connolly and Plunkett. The Barracks proper, i.e., accommodation, marching squares, training areas and dining halls were situated between the Top Road and the Middle Road, while the family houses were located between the Middle road and Bottom road. Sometimes people from outside the Curragh found it hard to remember the new names for the barracks, calling them by their British names, i.e. Gough barracks etc. This annoyed my mother and she always corrected them.

Between Ceannt and Connolly Barracks, and on the Bottom Road were the Boys' and Girls' Schools—two very fine 2 story redbrick buildings, separated by a long corridor, with two playgrounds, one for boys and the other for girls. Each school had six large classrooms with very large windows and large hall-

ways, and cloakrooms where we could leave our overcoats—
and where all the gossip took place. Opposite the school, was
the swimming pool which for many children, was the most
important building in the Camp, This then was town centre in
our 'hometown,' the Curragh, in the thirties, and during World
War Two.

Chapter Two
Earliest Memories

Childhood memories going back to age three are comparatively rare. However, my memory of St. Stephen's Day 1931 when I was three and four months old is as vivid to me as though it were yesterday. Perhaps the reason this memory stayed forever in my mind, is because on that day I encountered new and frightening happenings.

It was the afternoon of St. Stephen's Day (Boxing Day) and the family was sitting around the fire in our parlour, a small room off our living room in which we played and stored our toys, (as the family got older this room became another bedroom). The atmosphere was warm and cozy—my mother sitting in her nursing chair on one side of the fire, feeding my eighteen- month-old brother Emmet, my two older brothers, Harold and Sean sitting on the floor on the other side, playing with their present from Santa, a Meccano Set. (Each had their own – no favoritism).

I was sitting in the middle in my little chair, completely entranced by my new doll, whose eyes could actually open and close, and who could say ba-ba when I turned it forward. I had never seen anything like this before. From the gramophone in the corner, enveloping this peaceful scene was the beautiful voice of John McCormick singing "Mo Cushla."

Suddenly this cozy picture was shattered. An argument had broken out between 7-year-old Harold and five year old Sean, about where to hang the cranes in their Meccano sets. The argument intensified, and the shouting increased, both brothers deaf to Mammy's warning to behave.

In a moment of frustration she jumped up to intervene. She thrust Emmet into my arms and went to separate the other two. Emmet wasn't happy about being interrupted during his feeding, and tried to wriggle out of my arms. He almost succeeded however, and in trying to save him I tightened my grip and both of us fell towards the fender. By cradling him close to my body I landed on my left elbow, hitting the brass fender.

I remember the pain was excruciating, but my brother was unhurt. I became the heroine of the hour--by my quick thinking I had saved my brother from a horrible accident. But my adventures for that day were not over.

Wearing my new red Christmas coat, left arm exposed, I was taken to the Curragh Military Hospital—for me a new and very daunting place. After an X-Ray in the Emergency Department, it was confirmed that I had a 'compound fracture of the funny bone' (I never forgot this description). All the people I met in the hospital said what a brave little girl I was, and that I had saved my brother's life by hitting my elbow on the fender, and not letting him fall on the hearth.

It was a very nasty compound fracture, and I was the centre of attention for nearly 3 months. After the initial treatment, and when the fracture began to mend, as part of the extended therapy, I had to carry a bucket of sand in my left hand every day. I was also given a soft ball, which I had to press, seemingly to exercise my fingers. (See photo)

I still remember Dr. McInerney who was at that time Chief Surgeon in the hospital, and who it was said, saved the use of my arm. He was a special hero of mine for the rest of my life on the Curragh. My thanks to him and I hope he is carrying on the good work 'up there'

Chapter Three
EARLY YEARS

When we were young my two older brothers looked after the younger ones. Our pram was always full, mostly with two babies, one each side and, of course, bottles of water and jam sandwiches. My brothers refused to wheel the pram. They said it was a girl's job and therefore this very serious occupation fell to me, even though I could barely see over the handle bar.

However, it was well worth the effort, because we travelled all over the plains, and into Brownstown and Suncroft, where we picked blackberries and collected birds' eggs. Once we encountered a traveller-but in those days we would have called him a'tinker'-who was camped in a tarpaulin tent on the side of the road near the cross roads leading to either Cutbush, Maddenstown or Suncroft. He taught us how to make tin cans and a 'phony'. We felt nothing strange about sitting down near his tent. He had a head of black hair (quite like artists of today) and he seemed happy for us to be there.

There were some shops in the Brownstown area, a grocers shop and a sweet shop as well as , Williams, a Pub on the corner which was frequented by the soldiers from the Curragh as well as my father at different times. I think he preferred to drink away from the canteens on the Curragh even though the prices were lower. About a mile on the right was Maddenstown and in this area lived three horse-trainers, two of whom were Parkinsons and Collins. The third, of course, was the Aga Khan who owned a large farm nearer to Kildare and where we sometimes pushed the pram to 'Podgers' who were, if I remember rightly, in charge and where we bought eggs and milk. There was always great excitement during Irish Derby Week because the Aga Khan during the thirties, sometimes attended the races with his friends. My mother and her friends always paid a visit to the races as soon as word went round that he was in attendance. They gossiped about the glamour for weeks on end especially if they had seen some Hollywood actresses, hence the happy memory.

It was around this time that I got a present of a 'fairy bike.' I think possibly it was from my 'Communion Money' it took me a while to learn how to ride, because there was no such thing as stabilizers in those days. But my two brothers being older encouraged me to 'get up' and 'start again' and the three of us would end up racing around the Camp on our bicycles. The roads were really very well constructed and had no potholes. Consequently we became very good 'racers.'

Sadly, a 'complainant' (allegedly worried about our safety) went to my mother, and I regret to say this interference put an end to our racing skills.

Generally few people took notice of us in those days and we were free to roam about freely. We invariably joined up with other friends, both boys and girls, from school. We played marbles and conkers, The boys always preferred to play conkers with boys who claimed 'conkers five' and they also liked to play 'pitch and fall' with cigarette cards collected from cigarette packets.

One day my younger brother Emmet, got bored with playing conkers and marbles, and decided to take a ride on my bike. He had never ridden a bicycle before. The rest of us, totally engrossed in our games, failed to notice his disappearance. My mother was completely unaware of anything amiss until, answering a loud knocking on our door, she opened it to find Emmet, blood streaming down his face, in the arms of Danny Dunne, our local "Man of the Roads"

Danny was a victim of the trenches in the Great War, where he had been gassed and shell-shocked. This had left him with a morbid fear of being indoors, and I suppose nowadays he would be described as suffering from Post Traumatic Stress Disorder. However, in those days that term was unknown, and those suffering from this disorder were just ignored, and left to fend for themselves. Like many others, Danny took to the roads.

Unlike others who had no homes to go to, Danny had a perfectly good house in Brownstown where the family had lived for generations. But when I was growing up, Danny could be seen going and coming, tramping the roads and byways of county Kildare, and perhaps venturing into other counties as well. He had become a very solitary human being.

As youngsters we never quite understood him, and sometimes we would follow him and imitate his walk. When he came to Mass on Sundays he would sit, always in the same seat about three rows back from the altar, and in the centre of the church. We knew he was at Mass because he would 'plonk' his cap on the second seat in front, and the vibrations would echo round the church. This always made us giggle, but earned us some very black looks from our mother.

When my mother recovered from the shock of Emmet's accident, and talked to Danny she was amazed he knew where we lived. It was he who had found my brother on the Dairy Hill, where Emmet had attempted to ride the bike by freewheeling down the hill only to loose control as the bike gained speed. Mammy of course had to take him to the hospital where he was X-Rayed and the wounds on his face and lips required stitches. The scar is still noticeable today.

Of course, my beautiful bike was nearly a right-off, with the wheels buckled. However my father repaired both wheels and the bike stayed in use for a few more years. Eventually my father bought me a larger one, mostly for cycling to school.

After that episode we children were especially nice to Danny, and did not tease him--not that he seemed to notice or ever acknowledged our contrition. However he was always welcome in our house when my mother would ply him with cakes and homemade bread. But he would never come inside the house.

Around this time there was a Carnival in Kildare town. My mother encouraged my father to take my three brothers and me to the carnival by bike. So we all set off, me on the handlebar of my father's bike, Emmet on the back of my brother Harold's bike, and Sean riding his own small bike. The main attraction was the 'Stratosphere Girl. Everyone wanted to see this phenomenon, and we were very excited at this prospect as we cycled to Kildare.

It was so exciting, she climbed up and up towards the clouds, and we all clapped our hands as we encouraged her on. Looking back now, I don't think she climbed as high as our Spire on O'Connell Street, but it is nice to remember. After watching this event my brothers lifted me onto the 'swinging boats.' Perhaps the journey and all the excitement had made me nervous, but much to the disgust of my brothers I got sick. My father told them to take me home, I think we walked all the way home, minus my father. There were four of us and only two small bikes so you can imagine the humour of my companions!

In those days there were still some ruins left over from British Army days, particularly on the 'South Road.' There we discovered three sets of foundations, probably the remains of three houses, and here we girls played 'house'. We shared these with the Monahan's, the Whites and the Whelan's, spending hours during school holidays decorating our 'houses' and 'visiting' each other. My two brothers always vigilant, played next door with their friends, Ben and Orrie Wedick.

The Wedick's house was very large and their father had a batman/orderly, and they also had a live-in maid. There were stables at the back, and upstairs was a den, where they planned their 'cowboys and Indians' battles. There were other boys in the 'gang' including John McInerney (son of my favourite doctor), and I think they called themselves 'the Three Red Men'. The McInerney's lived beside the Wedicks, but Bubbles and Patsy McInerney thought our games too childish for them.

The four firing ranges, which occupied a very large part of this area, were used for army shooting practice. When we saw a red flag we knew we had to keep clear. We loved the South Road and I am sure some of our chennies' (pieces of glass) are still buried where we happily spent most of our summer holidays.

Not far from the South Road was the Brownstown Road. I think at that time the Transport Yard was situated a few yards down this road where horse drawn vehicles were housed at that time. I don't remember much about this area except a vague recollection of music and singing coming from there. The song 'Isle of Capri' played all the time (in later years I was to spend a few days in Capri and this brought back memories of the carnival). I often wondered in later years, whether, as word had it at the time, Gracie Fields had actually appeared at the carnival. I never knew for sure.

Nowadays there are rows of modern houses along this road, with families going about their business. I hope the children growing up there will have as good a time we had, growing up on the Curragh.

Our biggest adventure in those days was to follow the road north to Newbridge. I don't know why, but our mother declared this out of bounds. However our journey usually ended at 'Dead Man's Valley.' We never knew how this area got its name but the valley (now no more) was a source for snaring rabbits. This cruel way of rabbit-catching caused us a lot of grief, particularly when we saw see one caught in a snare. If the rabbit could not be reached and freed, then everyone ended up crying and feeling miserable.

Our next 'port of call' was usually the racecourse. This was close to Dead Mans Valley. Our mother never knew that we crossed the road to the racecourse after a race meeting. We did this to pick up race cards which we collected. However, we really were safe, and nothing untoward ever happened to use. After all my big brothers were in charge!

The sheep, as now, roamed all over the Curragh Plains, and a ranger was employed to look after them. However, some sheep managed to get through into the camp and it was not unusual to find them outside our door where we fed them with cabbage leaves.

As children the plains held a special place for us. There were no hedges, but encircling the Camp was an abundance of bright yellow and green sweet-smelling furze bushes. In the summer we used to lie on the grass in the warm sun, breathing in the beautiful scent.

We had the occasional curious sheep join us as we devoured our sandwiches, and drank from our bottles of water. We sometimes copied the sheep with their munching and chewing the grass.

Then we would try to outstare them, but the sheep still kept on chewing, and looking at us, and they always won the contest. Then, like most children, we eventually got bored and when we finished eating our sandwiches, we moved on, and roamed wherever we wished. However, relaxing with the sheep made us truly relaxed and happy.

The following poem from school really brings to life the memories of the sheep who looked upon us with sad and mournful faces:

> 'What is this life if, full of care,
> We have no time to stand and stare.
> No time to stand beneath the boughs
> And stare as long as sheep or cows'
> A poor life this if, full of care,
> We have no time to stand and stare.
>
> William Henry Davis

Chapter Four
EARLY SCHOOLDAYS

As we got older we began to realize we were different from the "townies" that is Newbridge or Kildare which were our nearest towns. It is hard to explain what we felt whenever we visited either town. We did, however, feel like comparative strangers, even when we eventually started secondary school in those towns. I started school a few months before my 4th birthday,

The Curragh School in those days was considered a large school, and the population in the thirties was perhaps the highest ever. When I began school, just before my 4th birthday there was no room for infants and high infants in the school proper. Consequently we were accommodated in the Gaelic Hall, a big yellow building opposite Donnelly Swifts, the photographer's shop, on McMurrough Hill.

Our teacher was a Miss Kenagh, and I remember her little primus stove on which she boiled water for her tea. Since then when I smell methylated spirits or paraffin, I think of her. Nowadays, to smell it in an Infant's Class would certainly cause a different kind of 'stink'! A Miss Dunne, later to become Mrs. Lawler, taught High Infants class. She was a modern day careers teacher, taking her career to the big school.

I am not actually positive, but I think I made my First Holy Communion from the Gaelic Hall.

Of course, even today this latter event is one of the most exciting periods for children. But when I was young it was even more so, not merely for us, but also for our mothers. As I was the first girl in our family to venture forth, from my mother's point of view my dress had to be the best.

Of course my mother made it. Besides her other skills, my mother was also an expert needlewoman. My dress for this solemn occasion was ankle length and trimmed with swans down (see photo). You might wonder, of course, where she procured this very fine trimming; it was, of course, from Todd Burns.

Moving to the big school for the start of First Class was a great adventure looked forward to with great excitement. The school was quite large for a primary school in the thirties. It had a separate area for boys and girls. The girls' playground was in very large yard within the school grounds. The boys had their playground in a field across the road. In the school yard there was also a lunchroom and bicycle shed. Usually we went home for our lunch, but if it happened to be raining my mother would surprise us with our lunch, and we looked upon this with great excitement.

The toilets were on two sides of the bicycle shed, girls on left, boys on right; the toilets all had plumbing and running water, and as far as I remember, were always spotlessly clean.

One of the senior boys in my day, Tommy Mooney, rang the Angelus Bell at noon in the yard every day, and the girls arranged to heckle him when he appeared, and put our tongues out -- we were really very nasty!

I think the school was extended round the late thirties. I have a vague recollection of this, because some of the bricks on the front were lighter than the rest.

Although the school was only about ten minutes walk from our home, my mother allowed me to cycle there. I used to give lifts on the back carrier to my friends. Alas, all my fun on this bicycle ended on my sister Bernie's first day at school.

I thought it would be a good idea to carry her on the back carrier which taking advantage of the hill close to the school. Speeding down the hill Bernie inadvertently caught one of her legs between the spokes of the wheel. So once more we had to go to the hospital casualty which resulted in Bernie having to have stitches just below her knee. Sad to say after this accident, my father sold the bike. Eventually he would buy me another, larger bike when I started secondary school in Kildare town.

As we neared end of the thirties I was continuing my education in primary school. At that time the Headmaster in the Boy's School was Mr. Sheehan. His nickname was "Baldy" –for the obvious reason. On the last day of term on the way out of school, and well out of the reach of the strap the boys used to chant—"no more Irish no more French, no more sitting on a hard auld bench, kick up tables, kick up chairs, kick auld Baldy down the stairs". The Head Teacher in the Girls' School was Mr. Sheehan's wife. She had a lovely dog called Bruno, so her nickname became "Ma Bruno."

The Curragh School had the reputation for having excellent teachers—and, without exception, they were. However, about the time when my older brothers were in the senior classes, there was a good deal of favouritism—old boy's network on a small scale. Because of some incident regarding school prizes, my mother eventually removed them from the Curragh School and sent them to CBS in Kildare town, and later to the De Le Salle Academy.

About this time too, when I was in fourth class, I don't think I was a bad student, but sometimes my mind would drift off, and occasionally I was quite nervous in the class. Often, I suppose, I made my teacher very impatient.

On one particular day, just after the summer holidays, my teacher was instructing the class about the central geographical features of Ireland. Truth to say I wasn't paying much attention-- I was more interested in watching a leaf falling from the tree outside. Our classroom was built on elevations, and my desk was in the top row which gave me a clear view through the large windows. However, from the corner of my eye I could see her bata fada travelling round the map, and part of my mind registered her words.

Sensing I suppose, that I was not paying attention, she called me down and told me to show the class what she was talking about. Of course, I knew exactly what she was doing, so I took the bata fada from her and, pointing to the map, I said that "the central plain of Ireland was like a saucer, a plain in the centre and mountains around".

I know there was a lot more, but under her glare I became very nervous, was unable to continue, and just went silent. This seemed to infuriate the teacher. She went to her drawer and pulled out another bata, (stick) referred to by us as the chair leg. It was a small thick stick which she used to threaten us when we were misbehaving.

This time, however, it was not just to threaten, but to use. In a fit of pure anger, the teacher hit me several times on my legs. The rest of the class looked on in shocked silence. The beating on my legs produced angry red welts, but I didn't notice, the pain and perceived injustice was almost too much to bear.

I cried all the way home, but pulled myself together when I reached the house and went into my bedroom. Of course I said nothing to my mother. In those days, children did not tell their mothers that they had been reprimanded or punished by the teacher. I felt she would have said it was my fault for misbehaving.

However, shortly after I got home, my friend Kitty Gallagher knocked at our door, and asked my mother if my legs were OK. My mother was taken by surprise, not understanding what

Kitty was talking about. She called me and looked at my legs. She was horrified at what she saw, and was furious at what the teacher had done. There followed huge rows between my mother, the teacher, and the school authorities.

So to cut a long story short, my mother removed me from the school sent me to the Presentation Convent, in Kildare town. I had just turned 11 years old. I had to travel to and from Kildare by bus. This was a little over 3 miles away, but at that time for me it seemed much further. I caught the bus opposite the church, and then we traveled along the Top Road, past Army Headquarters, and then on to the Gibbet Rath and into Kildare. I remember feeling a bit apprehensive, but at the same time very excited.

I have always been grateful to Kitty Gallagher for telling my mother about the beating, because this episode changed my schooldays and my outlook on life, and introduced me to what life was like outside the Curragh. Another benefit of this was that my younger sisters, this particular teacher treated Joan and Bernie, with kid gloves, and I doubt she ever took that "chair leg" to any child ever again.

Chapter Five

FAMILY LIFE IN THE THIRTIES ON THE CURRAGH

As the family expanded my mother got help from a lady called Sarah, who lived in Newbridge. She came once a week and she and my mother always had a great chat together. My mother always set dinner for her, and placed a packet of cigarettes and sixpence beside her plate. Sarah was a generous and warmhearted woman who never lost her temper with us.

She cleaned the house and made the beds, and afterwards she would move on to other homes. Though always patient with us children, she did not seem very interested in young people. However, Sarah never forgot us and as we got older and were studying in Newbridge, whenever we met her there, she would ask, with obvious affection, about my mother and all the family.

1932 (see photo) was the year of the Eucharistic Congress. Judging from this photo and what my mother told us, there were great celebrations on the Curragh. Our family is shown on the left hand side upstairs (five of us by then) and I think the Murtaghs and perhaps the Browns are there also. Around this time, or perhaps a year or so later, I remember a big snow storm and we were snowed in, and I can still can see a girl called Mary Doran coming through the snow. She used to help my mother with the children. I remember she taught me how to draw a house, and also helped me with my reading.

In one sense the families, or should I say, the mothers, were very lucky because most traders called to the door on different days.

Queuing was a word yet unheard, but would later become the bane of later generations. Of course, if I remember rightly, the traders were required to have passes from HQ.

Fridges in the homes were unheard of then. I remember milk was delivered every morning. In the summer evenings, we would cross the plains to Rowley's Farm where we got fresh milk and cream. We knew Doodles, who worked in the dairy. She milked the cows and worked very hard and took no nonsense from us.

Fish was delivered every Friday, and sometimes during the week as well. The breadman, and vegetable man called every day. Bacon Shops from Dublin brought oranges and nuts at Halloween and Christmas, together with a good variety of other Christmas fare. There was also a Mrs. Melee who came from Suncroft and sold sweets and lucky bags from her cart, which was pulled by a very old donkey controlled by her son, who was very surly, and never spoke to us.

As my mother always made her own bread we had to travel to near Suncroft to collect buttermilk. On our way home we invariably helped ourselves to a 'few' sips from the can. To hide the discrepancy, when we reached the pump at Brownstown we usually added some water into the can. My mother constantly threatened to have a word with 'Theresa' about her watery buttermilk. To this day I am not sure whether my mother was aware that we were the culprits.

The White Swan Laundry from Dublin called once a week but this facility was only used for sheets and bedspreads.

During my childhood we had a midwife named Nurse Kinsella. She was the grandmother of a family, the Gaffs who lived near us. I still can picture her, all in black, visiting families with her little black bag in which she," brought the babies to the mothers" as we were told. We never questioned this statement.

Eventually, a Family Hospital was opened, and most of the new babies were brought into the world there. Apart from this facility there was, of course, a doctor on call for any illnesses that might occur. The illnesses I seem to remember from those days were mostly mumps, measles, coughs, and colds. From what I can remember, most of the people, including the children on the Curragh, were a very healthy lot.

My mother always attended the jumble sales which were held every year in church hall of the Protestant Church. Being an avid reader she invariably came back with arms full of books. Our bookcases were always overflowing with books of all description. In days before television, most families, especially in the Curragh were avid readers, and in our house when we were indoors, we always had "our noses stuck in a book". I can still hear my mother's voice admonishing us when, indeed, she needed some help with the chores

Because my father was a mechanic and a driver, he was employed in the Corp of Engineers. However, he spent most of his army days in the Fire Station, where he drove the fire engine, and was also responsible for its maintenance. There were two engine drivers, my father and Mr. Smith. Sometimes they were called upon to attend emergencies outside the Curragh, and sometimes even outside the county. My father often spoke about the fire at the Carlow Sugar Factory, and of course we listened in awe to all his adventures.

My father had the reputation of being able to strip a car engine down to it's separate parts, find the fault, replace or repair the broken part, and put it all back together in a very short space of time. I often saw him with an array of engine parts on the ground, and before I knew it, the repaired engine was back in place, and he was driving off testing the car. When we were small we 'helped' him shine the brass fixtures (especially the bell) on the Fire Engine. He would lift us up, one by one onto the seat. That was, of course when nobody in authority was around.

Again, when we were small, my father used to take us to the stables in Plunkett Barracks, which was the Cavalry Corps, to see the horses. He loved horses. In later years he told us the story of how a colonel in the Australian army, whose family was originally from the same place as my father, had come to Ireland in 1911. He saw my father riding some horses, and seeing his skill, had advised him to join the British Army. We must remember that in those days before mechanized transport, the horse was an integral part of every army.

It was about this time that my father had had the big row with his father, and I suppose this gave him the impetus to leave home and join up.

I didn't like the smell of the stables, but I liked the horses and was always excited when he lifted me on a horse's back. My father told us that there were some really fine horses in the stables—I feel he really missed not being in more contact with these animals. Nevertheless, for me they could never take the place of sheep—but more about them later.

My father also kept about three or four beehives on the South Road, and we would watch the bees flying round the net and climbing up his arms. He never seemed to get a sting even when he lifted the honeycombs out of the hives. It was fascinating to watch.

He sometimes made toys for us. He made a big wooden rocking horse for my brothers, and a large dolls house for my sisters and me. But as the family grew in size he eventually gave up this occupation as it took up more of his 'off duty' time. He did, however, make a very modern pram later on. The family had already worn out three prams from constant use, and also as a result of all our adventures roaming around the Curragh. Later he confined himself to mending our shoes.

On the whole, most of the children living on the Curragh had been born there. As a result we knew every inch of the Camp from top to bottom, and any newcomer stood out. We had friends in all the different housing areas as far away as Plunkett Terrace and Pearse Terrace, and we had freedom to move throughout the area. All males, irrespective of their positions, were known to us as Mr. except of course doctors, and priests. All women were called Mrs. or Miss except nurses, who were also referred to as 'Nurse' or 'Sister'.

The Feast of Corpus Christi was celebrated every year with an outdoor Mass mostly in McDonagh Square. This was an outstanding event both for the army and the families. The girls were dressed in white dresses and veils, and the boys wore their First Communion suits. The Church Choir also sang, and during the Consecration the Army Cadets unsheathed their swords and the band played the Salute. I have to say it was a most impressive ceremony and etched in my memory to this day.

After Mass the congregation walked in procession around the Church headed by the first communicants of that particular year. In later years we also had our May Procession in honour of the Blessed Virgin and flower petals were thrown as the children walked in procession (see photo).

As memories take over I am reminded of our first dog 'Bunch'. She had a beautiful white fur coat and her tongue always seemed to hang from his mouth (see photo 1). All our friends loved to come and watch her – and were fascinated by the length of her tongue and often tried to measure it. The nearest they got was five inches.

When it was bath night Bunch was last, and she would be sent out to dry off. Alas, she mostly ended up rolling in the sheep's dung, or in the wet grass, and would come back covered in green. I think my mother had a lot of trouble with her over the years, but her puppies were in great demand. We missed her a lot when she disappeared, and she was also mourned by many of our friends. Later however, we were bequeathed a lovely dog called 'Teddy,' under life changing circumstances about which I will refer to later.

My father's greatest hobby was photography. When he was off duty it was rare to see him without his camera. Truth to say it disappeared at intervals, but my mother knew where it was— the pawn shop! Many of the photographs in this memoir were taken by him with his Kodak Diodak which had a 'banjo' front which we never got tired looking at. One of my favourite snaps was taken c1935 (attached) and includes five of my siblings, together with the Sheridan's (Paddy and Jim), Hughie Gallagher, and Sullivan from the bakery. I will refer to this happy photo again later.

Chapter Six
THE ARMY AND US

As I have already explained, there were seven barracks in the Curragh, all named after seven of the signatories of the 1916 Proclamation. (Later years we were always on top when this question came up in a quiz). The Army accommodated families in married quarters, in each of these seven barracks.

The family houses were in a separate part of the barracks from where the military were housed. There was very little contact between the children growing up and the military, per se. Of course, that was different with the military who were married and lived with their families on the Camp. In this instance growing up in this 'Island in the Plains' we knew every family, mothers and fathers from the so called 'top brass' to the ordinary soldiers, like my father.

The parade grounds, or barrack squares, were the only areas we were not allowed to enter. The squares were very convenient as short cuts to the roads above, and if we were in a hurry we sometimes took the risk and ignored this edict. However, quite often someone would see us and chase us back the way we had come, but at different times we managed to get through without being noticed.

As mentioned, the Irish Army was still in its infancy, but it had the advantage of having a very fine military establishment already in place in the Curragh. In the thirties each barracks had its full complement of soldiers. Every morning, in the distance we could hear the bugler call Reveille. As children if we were awake we would accompany him, chanting. *"come to the*

cookhouse door boys, when you're ready, fill your belly, come to the cookhouse door!"
There was always the 'last post' which we sometimes heard as we got older but it always sounded sad and now if I hear it I want to cry as it brings back some sad memories

The soldier's uniform in those days was a very deep green, made from coarse material. The tunic had a very high stiff collar with hooks and brass buttons down the middle. These buttons had to be shined daily with Brasso. I remember long leather leggings which came to below the knee. I think these were worn mostly by army transport personnel. During the Emergency the leggings were shortened to just over the ankle.

Every Sunday the soldiers were marched from their barracks to the church for Mass, and the army band played them back. When we were small children we "followed the band," but as we got older that was deemed unseemly by our mother, and was forbidden.

We loved the Band and tried not to miss their appearance in any function on the Curragh. From what I remember the Band took part in most festivities, including our Sports' Days. Of course, there were also big occasions, for instance when the Minister of Defence paid a visit. I vaguely remember Frank Aiken and Eamon de Valera inspecting the troop. On these occasions the band played a lot of classical music.

I have always loved classical music, and perhaps this was shaped from listening to this music from an early age. So I should like to offer my appreciation to the memory of the Army Band who played so beautifully. We also loved the marching songs they played, and knew all the words of each song, mostly because we learned them in School, thanks to Mrs. Sheehan who was very insistent that we attend singing lessons in every class. Needless to say, as an army band, they played a lot of patriotic songs and we children, with great gusto and feeling sang the words.

Chapter Seven
ENTERTAINMENT ON THE CURRAGH

Every year a seaside trip was organized for the altar boys and the church choir. Occasionally a few more children were allowed to accompany them, especially if their brothers were altar boys. A great help on these occasions was Peter Hickey who was the sacristan from the Church. He looked after everything, including the flowers, in the Church. He was as much a part of the Church and as important to us children, as the priests. He was there for our First Holy Communion, and for our Confirmations. Peter was a very nice man, was very popular and was respected by everyone.

Occasionally I was lucky to be picked to go on these trips. I even managed to get two trips, one to Portmarnock, and the other to Tramore. This was the mid thirties and the trips were very exciting for us. Mrs. Hughes, a member of the choir who accompanied us on the trips, always made us sing on the return journey. I remember one song in particular. It went like this *"horsey, horsey don't you flop, just let your tail go flipity flop...........we're homeward bound"* but we also sang all the popular songs of the time.

The greatest place of entertainment on the Curragh was, of course, the Picture House. This was situated on the corner on O' Higgins Road (the Bottom Road) at the bottom of the Dairy Hill. It was owned by Mr. and Mrs.Sylvester, and their son. To us it was a place of high adventure and during the matinees with every seat filled with excited children, the atmosphere was almost tangible with heady anticipation. During the film the children, with great gusto, joined in all the action verbally any way—and the noise inside the Picture House must have been tremendous.

We loved the cowboy and Indian films with Roy Rogers and Trigger, Tonto and the Lone Ranger, Tom Mix, and Gene Autry. Many of our cowboy and Indian games were based on these films, and for days afterwards the action was reenacted amongst the trees in the growing plantations, and on the plains. Around this time we were told that the great Roy Rogers and his horse Trigger, were coming to visit McDonagh Officers' Mess. When the great day arrived, my brothers took us to see this great cowboy and his famous horse. Not only did we see him, but also he actually spoke to us! I had my sister Irene, then just a baby, in my arms, when lo and behold the great man, saying some kind words to us, patted her on the head. Since then we never let her forget this bit of excitement.

While the boys loved the cowboy and Indian films, on the whole the girls, especially the younger ones, preferred films with Shirley Temple, Judy Garland, and Pinocchio. My favourite at the time was 'Snow White. It seems, looking back now that songs seemed to be sung in most films. One song stands out in my memory. It was from the film "South of the Border" with Gene Autry. I vaguely remember a rather sad film, But I do remember the song from the film *'South of the Border, down Mexico Way" That's where I fell in love,,,,,,,,etc.*" Of course, I have to admit, I was then about 13, and very romantic!

There were matinees on Saturdays and Sundays, but we could only go on Saturdays, unless an Aunt or Uncle paid us a visit. It was tuppence to get in but, with six anxious faces, what else could my mother do, so two days cinema going was out of the question. One year the children were entertained by a pantomime, which was held in the Picture House. All I remember of this is children shouting *"same man, different clothes"* which we had been prompted to say. But I can still remember the joy we children felt being part of the show.

Beside the Picture House was the bakery. This was a very large grey coloured building, with a great roller crane that hoisted sacks of flour up from the supplier's lorries. The smell of fresh bread was great, and sometimes we would be given a slice from one of the men working there. A family called Sullivan lived in a house next to the bakery and were known as "Sullivan's" from the bakery.

Roy Rogers was not the only famous person to visit the Curragh during this time. A few years earlier, in the mid thirties, we had a visit from the Great Dan O'Mahony, the World Wrestling Champion. A huge reception had been arranged in the Gym, which at that time was a big wooden building that had been built about 40 years before.

Dano had been a soldier on the Curragh, and was renowned for his sporting abilities, one of which was wrestling. He had been discovered by a sports promoter who arranged for him to be discharged from the army, to train professionally in wrestling, He ultimately became the World Champion. On a touring holiday in Ireland, he paid a visit to his old comrades in the Curragh. He got a great reception—it seemed as though every inhabitant had turned out to welcome him..

My mother brought us all down to the gym to see this great man. She was holding my brother Dermot, who was a tiny baby at the time. Walking through the crowds, Dano came near to where they were. He lifted Dermot from my mother's arms, and balanced him in his hand. Thereafter, to his friends Dermot was known as Dano, and even today he is still known outside the family as 'Dano'

Chapter Eight

SPORTS, AND THE END OF AN ERA

When I say everybody knew everybody else on the Curragh, we had good reason, and not only because of meeting in school. Sport was an integral part of our lives, and every summer each battalion held their individual Children's' Sports Day. Most of us children spent the spring and early summer months training for the competitions, all hoping to win prizes. Some really keen athletes, trained all year round.

At this time there were two sports grounds, one near Ceannt, behind Army Headquarters, and the other behind the priests' house. The latter was our favourite, as it had a fine green pavilion, beneath whose veranda we could shelter in the rain, and a viewing area in front where seats were set out on sports day for the visitors. There was also a bandstand where the band played. The sports pavilion was another relic of British Army days. This sport's field was very large, with sandpits for the long jump and high jump.

We participated in all kinds of athletics, but the high jumps and long jumps were confined to the boys. For the younger children there were three-legged races, egg races, sack races, backwards races, and 20 yards races. For older children the races were divided into under 14, under 16, and the rest over 16 considered adults. These races consisted of 50 and 100-yard sprints and 400 yards, and of course the relays in the different categories.

As a finale to the Children's Sports there was always a fancy dress competition. This entailed rummaging through boxes and wardrobes for anything we could find to make a costume, while at the same time going through books, magazines, and comics hoping to get inspiration.

I would say that there were about six Sports' Days during the summer, and all were very well attended both by the Army, the families, and the Army Band. And without boasting, our family did manage to win many competitions. The winning prizes were mostly medals, silver trophies, books, boxes of chocolates and big jars of sweets—the latter greatly prized by the younger winners. I remember winning a book, a famous classic 'A Tale of Two Cities' it was my first 'big' book I think I was about eleven and it took me a few years to appreciate what it was all about.

The following year I won a book that was an English Classic, which I found very hard to understand. As I recall, my book mentioned a ship that sank somewhere in the Pacific, and there were only two survivors a husband and wife who somehow managed to have a baby boy when they were marooned on 'the island of the apes' Later a film was made called 'Tarzan' about a plane crash in the jungle and Tarzan and Jane had a baby, and there was no Nurse Kinsella there either. It puzzled me for a long time how this came about. It was years later that I found out how a baby could be born without coming from Nurse Kinsella's bag.

Most of the girls at the time would have preferred a girl's book such as 'What Katie Did' 'Little Women' or 'Just William' but nevertheless 'a prize is a prize is a prize' and we treasured them.

My siblings still have some of the prizes they won at the Children's Sports.

Army Headquarters encouraged us to participate in every aspect of athletics. And now another sport was soon to occupy our lives. We were soon to enjoy swimming and diving at the newly refurbished swimming baths, which was later to become the home of the Curragh Swimming Club—a very special place in my memory.

In winter we continued playing outdoors. As in summer our playground was the Curragh plain, a wonderful place snowballing. Our favourite place in the winter snow was the Magazine Pond. When we were very small we believed all ponds were called 'magazine.'

However, the reason our pond was called this was because of the uncompromising building situated behind the pond. This was actually the arsenal depot where the ammunition was stored. We were unaware of this at the time as we played, in summer, splashing around in an old bathtub—but to us a pirate ship—and in winter on the ice.

When the pond froze over in winter we made various slides (owned by whoever got there first). Nobody had ice skates, so we just slid along in our boots—landing very often on our backsides. When the ice was thin or had begun to melt, there was always one or two of us who fell into the water. But the pond was only one to two feet deep and a wetting was worth the joy we felt.

Not far away from the Magazine, on the hill behind the priests' house, was where the real action took place. This sport was only for the older children, (now known as teenagers) boys and girls, because it was quite dangerous. As soon as the snow lay thickly on the ground it was time to start sledge racing.

We didn't have real sledges or toboggans. We used every kind of device we could find which sometimes included my mother's washing board to enable us to speed down the snow-covered hill. Our favourites were corrugated iron sheets, bent up in the front. On these 4 to 6 of us, clutching tightly to each other, could speed down the hill, at the bottom of which was a large bump over which we flew.

This was highly dangerous. The edges of the corrugated sheets were very sharp, and during collisions or falls could cause very serious injuries. At the same time, during very cold weather the hill became a sheet of ice, and the makeshift sledges sped dangerously fast, and sometimes capsized, causing broken limbs. The casualty and x-ray departments in the hospital became very busy at this time.

Because of these dangers, sledging on the Priests' Hill, as it was called, was strictly forbidden, by parents and the authorities. It was a common sight to see the PA chasing away the youngsters, and trying to confiscate their sledges. But on the whole, very few people paid a visit to the back of the priests' house in the icy cold winter, and the sport continued every year when we had good snowfalls. When the snow was gone, the makeshift sleighs were hidden away to be taken out the following year.

Even though life took me to more difficult slopes, I still remember the thrill, and pure enjoyment and happy laughter, coming from both places.

Part II

Chapter Nine
THE EMERGENCY AND EVACUATION

In 1939 there was great talk of war, at that time war meant nothing to us. Of course, we had our own wars in the history lessons in school. Every child knew about the Battle of Clontarf where our last King, Brian Boru died fighting the Vikings, Strongbow and the Normans and of course, the Battle of Kinsale. But in 1939 the history we learned in school seemed to stop with the 1916 Rebellion. Many of us knew, by heart, the names of all the seven signatories to the 1916 Proclamation and some could even recite the Proclamation. This was 'army life' and what we grew up with and were very proud to be living in the Curragh Camp.

We were to learn a lot more of our history, as we got older. However, in those days few people discussed the history of Ireland after the War of Independence, and certainly did not discuss the recent civil war. However, in September 1939, Britain declared war on Germany.

In September that year around about the time of my birthday, Radio Luxembourg shut down. That might awfully trivial in the face of events to come, but for us children, the wireless was our outlet to the outside world of music etc. The loss of this radio station was a great disappointment to us consequently listening to Radio Eireann became more important to us at that time.

The war, at first, seemed so far away. Little did we realize that this Declaration was to have a devastating effect on us, living as we did, in a military establishment..

In 1940 the Irish Government declared that Ireland would be a neutral country for the duration of the war. It also declared a State of Emergency within the country. This meant that the Irish Army was charged with securing the State against any incursion of a foreign power. To augment the standing army, a 'Call to Arms' went out to conscript new recruits. Young men from all over the country answered the call, and many of them were deployed to the Curragh. (see leaflet) I have a vague recollection of a new Unit being formed just before the Emergency, and the name of this Unit was the Construction Corp. (see leaflet)

This Corp wore a different uniform, I think it was grey/blue as distinct from the army green, and the men were very young, some seemed little more than children. They were later absorbed into the regular army for the duration of the Emergency. In order to cope with this large influx of recruits accommodation had to be found in the Curragh Camp. Finding billets for these young men became a huge problem for the army.

Shortly after the Emergency was announced, word came through from HQ that the family houses were required as accommodation for the new influx of recruits. This meant that all the families would have to leave their homes and move elsewhere – but where?

For the families, numbered in their hundreds, finding suitable homes in the county at such short notice would be well-nigh impossible. Most households had several children, as had the majority of families throughout Ireland at that time. Accommodating these families with relatives was difficult. Besides, the families had been used to their own homes, where very happy in these homes, and had no wish to intrude themselves on others.

My father being an 'army man' took this as a command and set about finding a suitable house in the neighbouring towns.

However, my mother, being 'civilian' refused the 'command' and was adamant she was not leaving! After all, she had a very good home which she had built up over the years. Apart from this she was expecting her 9th child at that time.

Adamant in her refusal, and judging from the arguments that followed this decision, my mother was not looked upon very favourably by the powers on high. But she remained steadfast to her decision. By this time the majority of the families, fearing the worst with the threat of war, left their homes hurriedly, and moved out of the Curragh.

I am sure my mother felt very lonely at that time, particularly as her best friend, Mrs.Monaghan and family (see family photo) had moved to Sligo. She was going to miss their weekly trip to Sandes Picture House. Much to my own disappointment I had to give up my music lessons with Mrs. Steadmon, as she and her family had also left.

There was also the Lynch family, who were very good neighbours of ours, who went to live in Kilcullen. Mrs. Lynch often brought us on trips with her own family, mostly to Fr. Moore's Well where we prayed. On most occasions we walked there, we did, however, cycle on occasions, as it was a long trek. The Holy Well was situated behind the Racecourse, and nearer to Milltown. The proposed evacuation was the first big upheaval I had experienced in my young life, and was something I have never forgotten.

We lost most of our playmates and friends. It was so traumatic it felt like bereavement, never to be forgotten. Among the friends we lost were the Murtaghs, the Sheridans, the Shaws, Sullivan's from the bakery, the Seerys, the Gallagher's, the Hughes, the Hargroves, the Caffreys, the Friar's, the Devines and many others. The Byrnes and McGowan's had lived on the Dairy Hill, near the Signal Corp, a very big impressive red brick building.

Mr. McGowan owned a car, and he often took us for a ride as far away as Ballytore, but they had also left.

The Cahill's from the Yellow Terrace went to live in Brownstown, so we still managed to see them sometimes, and we ended being lifelong friends. We had spent our formative years skipping, playing ball, relevio, cricket, hopscotch, and rounders.

When I hear the old childhood chants which we used to sing as we skipped,-----------

Apple Jelly my jam tart, tell me the name of my sweetheart, A, B, C, D etc.

All in together girls, this fine weather girls when I count 20 the rope must be empty

And played ---------------

In and out through the woods and blue bells my fair lady, counting and who should we marry - a Tinker, Taylor, Soldier, Sailor, Rich Man, Poor Man, Beggar Man, Thief, etc.

I'm Shirley Temple, I've curly hair, I've got two dimples, I wear my clothes to there..............

And when we 'fell out' with our friends --------------------

"Oh Lord above send down a dove with wings as sharp as razors..and send her to........"

By now we were alone in McDermott Terrace, with soldiers billeted all around us. It was very strange. However, scattered throughout the houses in the other barracks, were still a few families who, following my mother's 'standoff', had refused to leave. After all, they too had nice homes with running water, indoor toilets, and electricity. At that time, 1939/40, there were very few available houses in the county that could come up to those standards.

Army Headquarters must have been in a dilemma, and possibly unsure of the best way to handle this 'rebellion'. Eventually they capitulated, and the families remaining were moved to the eastern end of the Curragh, to Pearse Terrace. We were heartbroken to move from our house, and felt a great loss.

Pearse Terrace was a long way from the shops, schools and church, and away from the civilian area which we knew so well. For Harold, Sean and I it meant a much longer walk to the bus stop where we caught our bus to school in Kildare. Amongst all this upheaval, I was also in transition in school.

Chapter Ten

SECONDARY SCHOOL

Time was marching on now and my two older brothers were studying for their Inter and Leaving exams at the De La Salle Academy. I was too young for secondary when I finished primary, but at the time our school had what was called the 'technical class' and I passed into this. I suppose it was a kind of transition year, prior to going to Secondary.

The curriculum included, cookery, bookkeeping, typing and shorthand as well as the other subjects. Examinations in the commercial subjects were recognized by the R.S.A. from where I managed to get two certificates in junior bookkeeping and typewriting. The nun who taught us these subjects was called Sr. Bernadette who was very popular with all the pupils.

The following year I started in Secondary school and was very happy, but I missed the commercial subjects. However, I settled down and started studying for the Intermediate Examination.

By chance I was listening to Donacha O'Dulaing some weeks ago, where some person remembered the Cocoa Hall. Talk about déjà vu! I remember it very well—not for the cozy connotations, but for more serious matters.

I was with three other girls, charged with giving out cups of cocoa, and generally looking after the little ones. Suddenly one of my classmates pulled out a cigarette and lit up. She offered each of us a pull—which of course we accepted—to do otherwise would have branded us as sissy.

The Cocoa Hall was a long corridor at the end of which a short flight of stairs led up to the kitchen. The children drank their cocoa on seats near this end. That day a cookery class was taking place. Our smoking session was rudely interrupted when the kitchen door flew open and Sr. Anthony appeared, face blazing. Apparently the cigarette smoke had penetrated her kitchen.

We were marched up to Reverend Mother Dominic and severely reprimanded; perhaps that is why I never smoked.

Educating her family was proving a great strain for my mother, because by 1941, my third brother Emmet, was at the Academy. That meant that money had to be found to pay for four school fees. In the weeks preceding the new term, this subject was always on the agenda. But being the person she was, our mother continued to make sacrifices, and did not complain unduly.

Occasionally however, she did show some annoyance when we needed our bus fares. Although earlier on we used to cycle, our bikes had by now deteriorated, and needed a good deal of repair. I can still visualize my mother, putting our weekly bus fares, which amounted to 2 shillings—four pence a day for each one, into our hands, This was a lot in those days for bus fares. However, I think my brothers were able to help with this dilemma.

At this time, during the holidays and at weekends, they had jobs caddying at the Golf Links. A great part of the tips they earned went into the family budget, and helped pay the school fees, and the bus fares. However, in 1942 the old wooden Club House caught fire. Temporary accommodation was found for the Club House, and in 1944 the new Club House was built. There was a shortage of golf balls after the fire, and we were all asked to look out for lost balls. The boys mostly did this, and I think they were paid for each ball handed in.

When we moved house to Pearse Terrace I had to get up much earlier to catch my bus to Kildare. The most difficult part for me at that time was walking along the road to the bus stop.

In my early teens now, I felt acutely embarrassed as I had to pass the billets of the young recruits, some not much older than myself.

Their living quarters were now located on both sides of the road, and, like all young men at that time, they whistled incessantly when any girls passed by. I felt acutely embarrassed, and dreaded having to walk down that part of the road. After a while I got used to it in the mornings, as I was generally in a rush to catch the bus.

It was much harder coming back after school, but I discovered another road down by the Gym, McMurrough Hill, near the Military Hospital. This was a longer journey, and besides avoiding the cat-calls of the young recruits, it was a much more interesting route for me, because I passed some really attractive buildings, including the Military Hospital and the Nurses' Home and the Doctors' Home.

These three buildings that formed the main part of the hospital complex, were particularly fine buildings. The Military Hospital was a very large red brick Victorian building, with a flight of broad steps leading to the imposing entrance doors. When I was growing up I loved this building. It looked so majestic and permanent. When the sun shone one had to stand and admire the picture, and everything seemed much more peaceful and tranquil. The other two building were of similar design, but much smaller. Dr. Kelly lived in his own house in he hospital grounds with his wife and daughter Joan.

However, one day on my way home from school about January 1941, this tranquil picture was shattered. As I passed down the hill, I saw several ambulances at the casualty entrance to the hospital, and many people milling about. It seemed as though there had been a very bad accident somewhere.

When I got home I learned that there had been a major tragedy on a beach in Co Wexford. Four Irish soldiers were killed while trying to destroy sea mines that had washed ashore. At that time, in their efforts to stop ships from America and Canada bringing vital food supplies to Britain, the Germans had laid sea mines around the British coast.

These sea mines were often washed up on Irish shores. To protect the people and property in these areas, the army was constantly on the lookout for these devices to deactivate them. These four brave soldiers were trying to do this, when the mine exploded, killing all four.

That evening we were told that Mr. Curran had been killed. We were all shocked and very upset, as we knew the Curran family very well. They lived beside the school, and my brothers knew the Curran boys, William and John, and Kathleen, the only girl, had been in my class in the Curragh school.

The other three young men were all from around the Curragh, and had joined up at the Emergency to protect their country. My brothers said that and one of them, Joseph Tinsley was the son of Mr. Tinsley, who was in charge of the Greens at the Curragh Golf Club. This tragedy resulted in a period of deep sadness and gloom that permeated the whole Camp. Often, when walking past the hospital on my way home from school, I would think about these brave men.

This was the second tragedy that had struck Co. Wexford. The year before, German aeroplanes had bombed the village of Campile, killing several people. The German ambassador in Dublin had apologized for this 'dreadful mistake'. Several bombs had been dropped in different parts of Ireland in 1940-41, including one at the Curragh Race Course. These bombings had resulted in deaths, but claimed by the Germans as mistakes. But people lived in fear of more 'dreadful mistakes' and grew more worried about the protection of the country.

Their fears were not groundless, because later in May 1941 the Germans attacked the North Strand in Dublin, killed 34 Irish civilians, and wounded 90, prompting again, more apologies from Nazi Germany. This of course added to the tension on the Curragh, and added impetus to even more intensive training of the the Irish Army.

It also brought the war much nearer home.

Chapter Eleven
OUR NEW DOMAIN

In the past we had rarely visited Pearse Terrace, which was situated on the eastern side of the Camp, so we hardly knew the area in which we were now living. The one exception to this was the road leading east to Athgarven and Donnelly's Hollow. In the summer when the weather was hot and sunny, my mother used to take us on regular picnics to the River Liffey near Athgarvan. There we paddled and played in the water all day 'til the sun went down. Sometimes my father, after work, would cycle there and set up the primus, and we enjoyed hot tea with our sandwiches.

As we grew older we became very good swimmers, which was an asset when the Curragh Swimming Club was started. By that time we could go on our own to the river, we preferred to go to a place called Butcher's Island—I don't know how it got this name. This was in Kineagh, near Kilcullen, and was on Lady Blacker's estate. (see photo) We were trespassing of course, but we somehow avoided getting into trouble on most occasions, especially if we let Percy Blacker join us.

It took us a long time to settle down in Pearse. But there was one good thing about the evacuation – we got our dog 'Teddy,' a wheaten terrier. Teddy was given to us by the Hargreaves. They didn't want to move him as he was getting older. He knew our family well, so when he came to us, he helped to cheer us up. He became our best friend, and a reminder of our friends who had left their homes so reluctantly.

In hindsight I believe they must have left in a state of panic, thinking we were going to be bombed – my mother always said it was the safest place in Co. Kildare. The army would have to build air raid shelters and perhaps underground bunkers where we would be safe. Indeed the army did build these within a few months. (After the Emergency these shelters made great 'camps' and hideouts for the various rival 'gangs')

As time went by we did manage to make new friends, and I was still of an age when I could ramble around the area. My older brothers did not go about with us very much now, as they were studying for exams, and in their spare time, caddying at the golf links. Now, being the eldest girl, I was in sole charge of the younger ones.

For now we were confined to the eastern end of the Camp, as distinct from the 'town centre.' We still passed through the camp to get to the church, the larger shops, the schools, the Picture House, and of course, for the older children, the bus to school. These places were a long walk from Pearse. We had to get us much earlier now, and early in the morning our house was a hive of activity—washing, getting dressed, and of course, eating our breakfast. We were never allowed to go to school without eating our breakfast.

But I think, for us teenage girls, the worst part of walking through the Camp was running the gauntlet of the young recruits, as they whistled and called out from the windows of their billets.

We were all very naïve and unsophisticated, and our parents strictly forbade us talking to these young men. Our lives revolved around school, exploring the plains round the camp—children of all ages roaming together, sports practice, and of course, swimming.

We now had new areas to explore, and, as always the pram was taken out, and we lost no time in setting off. First, we found the golf links and second, Donnelly's Hollow. The latter was of more interest to us, because there was a monument in the hollow commemorating a great boxing match between the great boxers, Donnelly and Cooper—I think the monument said in 1815.

Of course, in this famous match, Donnelly, the local hero, beat Cooper, his English rival. What really fascinated us children, however, was the story that Donnelly's arm had been preserved, and was actually on display in a pub in nearby Kilcullen. We never saw it of course, but in our imaginations the arm took on gigantic proportions and powers, while at the same time, was very creepy, being the arm of a dead man!

Running down the side of the Hollow was a line of footprints known as Donnelly's footprints, apparently made by him as he ran down the hill to meet Cooper. Through so many people walking in these footprints, they had now become permanent holes in the ground. We added to their size by spending our time running up and down, copying Donnelly, until we fell, or got bored.

The area around Donnelly's Hollow was very hilly. Cloaking the hills were masses of bright yellow furze bushes, which could be seen for miles around. They produced the most amazing scent that permeated the whole area. This scene continues to be a beautiful picture in my heart to this day. Of course in those days, we took all this beauty for granted, and for us this area was ideal for playing hide and seek.

Another big historical monument around this area was the entrance to the old British Graveyard. We spent a lot of time walking round the graves, and saying prayers for the dead. One day with my baby sister in the pram, and I of course, 'in charge' of the three younger ones, we set off on our usual journey, 'exploring.' One of our destinations included the Old Graveyard, where we carried out our usual routine of reading the names on the gravestones, and saying our prayers.

When we got home my mother, taking the baby out of the pram for her feeding, found a 'little angel' among the blankets. It appeared that unknown to me, one of my young sisters had taken it from a grave, and hid it in the pram. My mother was horrified, and of course, I was blamed for not keeping a closer eye on my sister. I was ordered to take the 'little' angel' and put it back on the grave.

I think I cried all the way back to the graveyard, hoping that nobody would see me doing the 'deed' This episode reminded me of Christmas a few years earlier, when Peggy Kelly who lived in Ceannt Terrace, climbed into the Crib and made off with the Baby Jesus. She must have been only about seven years old, and the Baby Jesus looked like a lovely doll. I don't remember if anything untoward happened to Peggy, but the Baby Jesus was soon back in its Crib. We had beautiful life sized statues in the Crib, and I hope, that every Christmas, they still form that nativity scene.

My brothers were now getting older and were allowed to 'caddy' on the Golf Links. The money they earned in tips, I believe, made a big contribution to the family budget. Once a child reached 16, my mother's army allowance was reduced. Through the war years, girls were also allowed to caddy as there was a shortage of older boys. I never had the 'pleasure' as I was needed for household chores, and looking after the younger children.

We were always on the lookout for another 'South Road,' an Eldorado for us, and we found one! In our exploration east of the camp, we came across what became known as Fahy's Wood. This was situated on the Green Road—the back road, to Newbridge, and was quite near the Sentry Box at the eastern entrance to the camp. A family called Fahy, whose father was a local doctor, had lived there in the past. The children were much older than we were, so we didn't know them very well. I can barely remember their father or mother.

The house had been a very pretty bungalow, the wooden exterior painted red, with a white-painted veranda all around. It had been set back in a lovely garden with a large water fountain. After the family left the Curragh, their house was demolished. However, the foundations were still there, and it was here we set up 'house'. Of course, these foundations were neither as nice nor as extensive as our previous 'houses,' on the South Road.

It didn't matter, because to compensate, there were apple trees and other fruit trees, as well as gooseberries and raspberries. The smell of the apple blossom will always remind me of those days spent playing in that beautiful place. There were several lilac trees, and in spring we used to bring handfuls of the blossoms home, and their beautiful aroma scented our house for weeks. Besides all these great finds in Fahy's Wood, we also discovered a freshwater spring. The water was clean and pure, and cupping our hands, we drank deeply. When we had our picnics here we didn't need the bottles of water.

Alas, our fun was cut short when the army confiscated the area, for maneuvers and army training. But with the ingenuity of childhood, we changed our tactics, and found new games to play. From a safe distance, and hidden away where we couldn't be seen, we watched the recruits going through their training activities.

When they left and returned to barracks, we took over the area and copied everything we saw the soldiers doing. We climbed the wooden frame, walking our hands across the top, and swung from the ropes pretending to be Tarzan. And best of all, we used the moving boards the troops used to run across, as 'swinging boats'—all of us clinging together as we swung the wooden boards higher and higher, while we listened to the heavy iron chains creaking the faster we went.

Sometimes, copying the soldiers we would race each other across the moving boards. We thoroughly enjoyed the fact that we could climb the props and 'anything they could do we could do better.' This had become our favourite place to play.

The games we played in the training ground were quite dangerous for youngsters, but I don't remember anyone breaking bones, or having other major accidents. I'm sure had the powers that be known where we played; they would have been more vigilant in watching the area to prevent this happening. As the area was surrounded by trees and shrubs, the PA in the sentry box further up the road seemed unaware of our existence.

However, on our way home we had to pass this sentry box, and I wonder now, where the PA thought we had come from. Perhaps buoyed up with our strenuous exercise and feeling of bravado, we often became very cheeky. Then we would make faces at the PA in the sentry box, and run away. We knew full well he couldn't follow us. But on the whole, the PA s took it in their stride, didn't take umbrage, and just smiled at us. They knew we were generally well-behaved children having a bit of fun.

Chapter Twelve
FAMILY LIFE DURING THE EMERGENCY

To their great credit, the army authorities did their best to keep us occupied and make us feel happy. Besides our usual swimming galas and children's' sports, they organized children's ceilidhes, gymnastics in the gym every Saturday, showed children's films of the time, like Banbi, and Dumbo the Elephant. At Christmas there were the Christmas Tree Parties, on one day for boys, and on another for girls. These events were greatly anticipated, with sandwiches and cakes and lemonade, and each child received a present from Daddy Christmas.

There were concerts for grown ups, and a good many famous people came down to perform. In the early years I was deemed too young to attend, and during the period of the Emergency, I was probably present at only two concerts. I have a vague recollection of attending a concert with my mother in which Delia Murphy sang. I think she sang 'The Spinning Wheel'

My mother always found it difficult to cope with tea rationing and like the song went:

'Bless DeValera and Sean McEntee for giving us the brown bread and the half once of tea................'

In order to stretch the tea ounces she would sometimes send us out to pick nettles. These she dried in the oven, and then mixed the dried nettles with the used tealeaves. Today nettle tea is becoming very popular as a health drink. But I believe nothing could compare with our nettles which grew in such abundance, mostly round the areas where we played. But perhaps also none could compare with the stings they produced! However, we had our own cure for the sting, it was, of course, the dog leaf from another plant which grew right beside the nettles.

Most of us were aware of the shortage of fruit, especially bananas and oranges, which were unobtainable in Ireland from 1939-1946. In order to fill our school sandwiches my mother cooked parsnips, cooled them, mashed them, and added sugar and banana essence. These were our banana sandwiches, and in those days we really enjoyed their taste.

The only thing, the brownish coloured bread which was sold in all the shops during the war was awful—everybody hated it. Fortunately my mother made most of the household bread. This was soda bread, with both white and brown flour. Sometimes it was baked in the oven, at other times on the grill. But we had to use the shop bread for sandwiches.

The army had their own grocery stores, where we could do our weekly shopping, and our weekly rations. My father usually took care of this chore, (as the cost of the groceries and the meat from the abattoir, was deducted from his pay, he was extra careful in how it was spent!). We got the bulk of our meat from the military abattoir. This was situated past the Golf Club on the way to Athgarvan. Sometimes in our rambles we used to go and see the cattle in the yard. We were always sorry for them because they had nothing to eat, so we used to gather grass and feed them through the wire fence—that is, until someone chased us away.

The abattoir was open on Tuesdays and Saturdays. It supplied beef, but no other meat. The meat wasn't rationed. I remember we used to get a large piece of beef, half of which was roasted for Sunday lunch, and the rest made into corned beef, which we ate a few days later. The leftovers from the Sunday roast were always made into shepherd's pie on Monday. My mother also cooked ox tails, and stuffed roast hearts.

We had chicken very rarely, and only on special occasions. It was always roasted and stuffed. When we had roast chicken, each of us got only a tiny amount of meat as a chicken did not stretch far for eleven hungry mouths, but the stuffing made it go further. Like everyone else we ate fish on Friday, and sometimes on Wednesday. My father had vegetable plots where he used to grow potatoes, carrots, cabbage, Brussels sprouts, turnips, onions, and rhubarb. In the summer we always had plenty of lettuce and scallions. So we had a plentiful supply of fresh vegetables. We were also very lucky in that we had blackcurrants and gooseberries growing in the vegetable plots.

In those days, all the mothers had their own, probably identical, agenda for the week. I don't think this agenda was adhered to in later generations, including my own. But I remember then it was washing on Mondays, ironing on Tuesday if the clothes were dry, and on Wednesday making soda bread and scones. On Thursday my mother and her sister, my Aunty Chris, went out to Suncroft for buttermilk. Friday was her day off and she invariably visited my aunt and ended up at the 'pictures'

About 1941/2 my brother, Harold, joined the LSF, the Local Security Force, later called the Local Defense Force or LDF. We were all very proud of him. Some people called the LSF 'the chocolate soldiers' because of their uniform which was made from very stiff brown coloured material. They wore caps of the same colour and most of them wore this at a jaunty angle on the side of the head. I am not sure what they did in their training, but he was always exhausted when he came in at night. My mother used to have a big meal waiting for him because he was also studying hard, and had to get up in the morning for school.

Of course, the troops were now everywhere. The sound of marching feet had always been a part of our growing up, but during the war the sounds were even stronger. The four Firing Ranges were now very busy places, and when the red flags were hoisted, we kept our distance. We could quite easily get caught in the crossfire. After the firing stopped and the soldiers had returned to barracks, we children would rush to the area to collect the spent bullets. These we used to barter with the boys who collected them.

Later in the Emergency the movement of children in the vicinity of the firing ranges became very restricted. This was because of my youngest brother, who was only about 3 years old at the time.

I was at school so was not involved in what happened. But I learned about it when I got home.

It seems several of the children, including the toddlers, had gone together to the firing ranges to collect the bullets. On the way home my little brother, Donal, as usual, was lagging behind. Nobody took much notice only to check that he was still following them. My mother watching out for their return, saw Donal lagging behind, and went to meet him. The reason he was slower than usual was because there he was, nonchalantly dragging a rifle bigger than himself that he had 'found' at the rifle range! I don't remember who was 'in charge' that day, but I remember being very glad it wasn't me! We never found out what the outcome was over this serious incident but I believe it was 'hushed up' and not spoken about again.

We still continued with our adventures, and our pram always seemed to be full of children's clothes, sandwiches, and bottles of water. By now we had explored all the places that we were interested in on the eastern end. One day we decided to explore further along the Green Road, the back road to Newbridge.

We had never previously passed the cross roads at the Drogheda Memorial Hospital, but that day the spirit of adventure encouraged us to keep on going. It was a lovely day, and we sang and imitated the bird songs. We had travelled about a mile when our dog Teddy ran from us and ran into a farmer's field and disappeared.

We called out and went in search of him but he was nowhere to be seen. We waited for about half hour, but he failed to return to us. We got very distressed, and it took me a while to quieten the younger ones so that we could go home. By this time we were all crying including me. I had the added burden of worrying what my mother would say-- after all I was in charge, and as usual felt the blame would fall on me. The hardest thing about this incident was that Teddy knew sheep and was not known to have troubled them in the 12 years of his life on the Curragh.

When we got home my mother questioned us and wanted to know exactly where Teddy had disappeared. Somebody was sent out to search but could not find him. After two days missing, needless to say, we gave up hope of ever seeing him again. On the third day my mother was standing at the kitchen window gazing out, when she saw a paw coming up the step in our back yard. It was Teddy.

My mother ran out and picked him up. She found him covered in blood, and whimpering pathetically. She carried him into the kitchen and laid him on his blanket. It was then discovered that he was bleeding from a neck wound. It was soon obvious that the wound was the result of being shot. She found several shotgun pellets embedded in his neck and infection had started in the wound. It was an awful sight, but my mother cleaned the wound and bathed it with iodine, covering it with one of her good pillowcases she had just taken off the cloths line. There was great excitement when the news got round that Teddy was home. Later my mother got some strong antiseptic ointment from the pharmacist in the hospital to dress Teddy's wounds, and eventually they healed.

My mother was very upset about what had happened, especially when the dog was well known and had no history of worrying sheep. Besides, to do such a thing in front of children was unpardonable. She made enquiries was told that the farmer was within his right to shoot a dog if he found it upsetting his sheep. As far as I can remember, my mother sought legal advice on the grounds that the farmer should have made sure that Teddy was dead, as it turned out he suffered terrible agony for three days before making his way home. My parents didn't have the means to pursue the case, and therefore this episode became a sad part of our growing up, and it was never forgotten.

Teddy survived the attack for about another two years and had to be put down because of old age. You came a long way Teddy!!! (See photo) We did, however, get another dog called 'Rover' a very intelligent mongrel, but to the older members of the family Teddy was 'our' dog Loosing him made us remember our friends from McDermot before the 'emergency,' but the pain was part of growing up and we learned to cope.

The farmers around the Curragh found it harder to get help to bring in the harvest. A call went out for help to bring in the fruit, strawberries, and raspberries. My friends and I took our bicycles, and cycled to the fruit farm, where we were asked to start the next day. It meant, of course, rising at about 6am and cycling about five/six miles to begin work at 8pm. It was very hard work, but it was summer time, and we were on school holidays and were getting paid.

We did make some money and my mother was very happy with the monetary help, and I had my first 'permanent wave' which I lived to regret. After two summers it changed for me as the farmer decided to get more help, and made a lorry available for anyone interested in the work. My mother refused to let me take the job, as I would have to go in a lorry. She considered me too grown up to be stepping up on a lorry. She was right of course, as the whole picture had changed and the fun had gone out of this adventure.

As time went on tension in the camp began to grow and the children were aware of this. By all accounts at this time the army authorities were becoming very conscious of the open spaces of the Curragh plain, and the fact that the enemy could infiltrate the camp. Therefore, they introduced stricter rules, and we were told not to talk to strangers,

I suppose because we children knew every inch of the Curragh Camp, where the different battalions were housed, the location of the armories, the names and ranks of important people, and in most cases where they lived. This made us feel very important and we took this 'command' very seriously.

Another edict that came from Headquarters at this time was the total ban on taking photographs anywhere in the Camp. Of course, photographs taken inside Donnelly Swift's studio were allowed. The last photograph my father took was on Corpus Christi in 1941. The next photographs he took were in 1946.

Besides all these external events, the Camp authorities had other problems of security to contend with, right here in the Curragh—the prisoners of war, or more correctly, internees.

Chapter Thirteen

FOREIGNERS AMONG US

About 1941 new names began to capture our imagination. These names were Tintown, The Glasshouse, and K-Lines.

Tintown and the Glasshouse, (Officially No.1 Internment Camp—though we didn't know it as that) was situated in the west side of the Curragh Camp. Members of the IRA were imprisoned there during the Emergency. When we heard people talking about Tintown and the Glasshouse, we were really curious to see these famous buildings. We were very disappointed when we recognized the dull and dreary buildings, near Sandes Picture House. And of course, there was no 'Glass' house! We quickly lost interest in this area—besides it was at the other end of the Camp from where we were now living, and not worth the long walk.

When I think back, I seem to remember that when the grown-ups mentioned the prisoners in these two places, they sounded very guarded as though uneasy about it. It seemed to have a very bad reputation. The only time we thought we recognized prisoners from there, was if we saw civilians arriving by ambulance at the hospital. Of course these civilians could also have been British or German prisoners.

Sandes Home, and Sandes Picture House near Tintown, were very popular establishments with the young recruits. The people who ran the place had the reputation for being very kind and hospitable to these, often very young and very lonely young men, away from home for the first time, but they were always assured of 'a cup of tea and a bun'. What a stark contrast it was to its neighbour, the sinister Glasshouse! I think Sandes Picture

House only opened at night. My one visit there was with my father, to see the film, Dracula. I can honestly say, that being too young at the time, I didn't enjoy it.

K-Lines, officially Internment Camp 2 was much more interesting for us, and I suppose for the grown-ups as well. This was where the British and German prisoners of war, or internees, were housed.

For us children it was a fascinating place. Remember, we had never seen foreigners before—meaning of course, the Germans. Not only that, but it was very near where we lived Pearse Terrace—in fact, just a short walk away. In the beginning we hardly saw any of the prisoners—I expect there were very few in the beginning of the Emergency. Later they became more visible, walking around the Camp, going to the swimming pool and the gym, and the Picture House, and going for walks along the Green Road. But to our great disappointment, the Germans looked like anyone else, except they were always very neat and tidy. Most of them seemed to have straight hair, combed back from their foreheads, with never a hair out of place

My younger brother Dermot said he had sneaked inside K-Lines. He was 12 or 13 then and was always up to mischief. The prisoners lived in huts, which according to Dermot, who claimed he saw inside, were very cozy, and had a wireless and a big stove to keep it warm. He made friends with some of the prisoners. Of course we were all sworn to secrecy, but we were really envious, and would have loved to have dared to sneak inside as well, but he would never tell how he managed to get in. However, I was now becoming more grown-up, and more and more relinquishing these childish activities.

One day Dermot came home, and his clothes were filthy. My mother was very angry with him—remember in those days we had no washing machine—and she asked him what had happened. He told her that it was the fault of "Hitler's Ass". It seems he and his gang, were coming back from Fahy's Wood, when they met one of the prisoners, who was out walking with his dog on the Green Road. The dog was huge, like a big Alsatian, and knew Dermot very well.

When he saw Dermot he raced over, jumped up on him and knocked him down on the wet ground, and started playing about, covering Dermot with mud. It transpired that the guards at K-Lines had named this dog Hitler's Ass—a name gleefully taken up by all the children—and I believe, the grown-ups too!

Dermot was very good at getting into mischief, but he was also very good at getting away with it!

It seems that inside K-Lines there was a wall dividing the Camp into 2 separate parts, one for the British, called B-Camp, and one for the Germans, called G-Camp. The German prisoners used to grow their own vegetables. Later on they used to work on the farms surrounding the Camp. They were also allowed to work on the bogs cutting turf. Early in the morning we could hear them singing and marching to work, and I think they were happy enough, and I feel sure they tried to make the most of their captivity

The German prisoners were always very polite, and seemed glad to see us children, and often stopped to watch us play rounders or cricket. Some were really good swimmers, and coached my brothers and the other boys. Others were often seen painting, mostly pictures of the landscape around the Curragh, but sometimes they would also paint the children. One of them painted a picture of the Green Road, and presented it to my mother as we were walking home from a day at the river. We have it still. After the war it was said that half of the German prisoners stayed on in Ireland, and made their homes here.

All the prisoners had to wear civilian clothes—in the beginning the Germans appeared very poorly dressed in comparison to the others. We knew the British Air Men by their clothes, to us, they seemed very well dressed. They wore fur boots, and leather jackets etc. and we considered them 'snobs.' The story was that they 'went through one gate and passed out through at another gate' and ended up in Belfast. But that may have been just a story at that time. But in truth it seemed very strange that prisoners of war were free to go and come as they pleased, and we often wondered why they all didn't run away.

Later I found out that each prisoner, in order to leave K-Lines had to make a solemn declaration which said--- *"I hereby promise to be back in the compound at (whatever) o'clock and, during my absence, not to take part in any activity connected with the war or prejudicial to the interests of the Irish state"*

Apparently they were free to move about if their first signed this declaration, and rather than jeopardize the chances for the other internees, they never tried to run away during their official time away from the Camp. It was sometimes said that some British prisoners had tried to escape 'legitimately' and some were caught and returned to K-Lines but others managed to get back to Britain... There were no American prisoners in K-Lines because the Irish and US governments had an agreement whereby these military were repatriated to the US.

The British internees were well treated, and also made friends with people in the surrounding areas. There were many Irish people in the nearby towns that did not agree with the government policy of remaining neutral and welcomed internees into their homes and allowed them to use their horses to go riding. The British internees had favourite places to visit, especially Lalor's Hotel in Naas, and of course, the Race Course. I heard rumors that there was a group who arranged successfully for some of the British prisoners to escape 'legitimately.'

About 1943 British airmen were no longer interned in K-Lines, therefore the Germans had the place to themselves. None of the

Germans escaped, and remained in the Curragh until the end of the war. But half of them decided to stay in Ireland, and several had already married Irish girls.

Looking back now, I believe it must have been the best place in the world to be as a prisoner of war.

Chapter Fourteen
SWIMMING AND OTHER SPORTS

As already mentioned the Army was very good to the families and made every effort to encourage our athletic and swimming skills. The opening of the refurbished indoor swimming pool was a great occasion for everybody. Now we could swim all year round, and we showed our appreciation by becoming good swimmers.

The pool was opened to all children at various times. For the school children that was after school, boys for the first hour and girls for the second. Our swimming instructor at that time was Mr. Broderick. He was very strict and if you didn't take swimming seriously you were ignored and left to your own devices. He moved around the pool shouting instructions but he never entered the water. But his training was relentless.

Every day we had to do several lengths, legs only, pushing the board, then several lengths arms only, and then sprints. We learned breaststroke, backstroke, and freestyle (crawl). As we progressed we specialized in the stroke in which we had become proficient and became good swimmers

We had children's' swimming galas once a year. The pool was 40 metres long and 20 metres wide, juniors (under 10) swam 20 metres, and seniors, depending on age, would swim 50 metres and 400 metres, in all three strokes. Then there were medleys, and also relays. There was also diving for plates and the swimmers, who emerged with the most plates, received a prize.

There were two diving boards, the lower one which was a springboard. The other higher looked very high to me at the time, and therefore I kept clear of diving. But I had great admiration for those who climbed the steps up to the diving board. (I wasn't a diver so I passed on this competition).

We were also instructed in lifesaving, and received certificates. The better ones also won medallions. My brother Emmet was a great swimmer and later, during the school holidays, he became a 'red coat' at Butlin's Holiday Camp. Soon after the re-opening of the swimming pool, the Curragh Swimming Club was formed. Most of us who were swimmers joined the junior section of the club.

We had some very good senior swimmers. One girl stands out in my memory. She was Kathleen McNally, and as very few of us had the same expertise, Kathleen always won first place in the crawl. At the time I was a junior member, on two occasions, our section competed in the Leinster Championships in Dublin.

The Army Benevolent paid our expenses on each occasion. The attached photo taken in 1946 at Blackrock Swimming Pool in Dublin shows our group. Between us we competed in the under 14. under 16 and under 18, The names from left are, Laurie McAteer, Joan Mullans, (cousin) Gertie Gaff, Joan McAteer, yours truly and Patty McRedmond. We also had our own swimming galas in the Curragh Club which gave us great confidence for future competitions.

Members of the army also competed in their own Gala at the Curragh Swimming Club. These competitions were always very well attended, and they were built around the prowess of a soldier in combat. Those competing had to wear full combat gear, with a rifle on their backpack. This was always an exciting race to watch, as some soldiers made it, and some stopped halfway.

It was great fun for the spectators and there was a lot of laughter from them. Army Certificates were also awarded for this event. There were also inter-battalion relay races, individual races in the different strokes and individual diving competitions, in which the contestants had to perform 4 different types of dive.

The older girls were also kept busy with the formation of a 'Ladies Camogie Club.' It was quite a big club, and they competed with other clubs round the county. I remember watching them play in Suncroft and Balitore. Their playing field was in the south side of the Camp, near the South Road. The sun 'sinking in the west' created a memorable picture against the shouts of encouragement from the spectators. The McCarthy, Whelan and Brick families were, I would say, the mainstay of the Club.

In the early years of the Emergency I was still young enough to compete in the 'Children's Sports' and I really enjoyed it. I have to say we were never bored as there was always something to do with the athletics and the swimming. Fancy dress competitions were still included at the end of Sports Day and all the children enjoyed dressing up.

I remember my brother Dermot got a prize for dressing up as 'Joe Lewis' wearing the boxing gloves he got from Daddy Christmas, and the shorts he wore for the sports. My sister Bernie got a prize for 'An tSean Bhean Bhoct,' with a shawl borrowed from the McGuinness' grandmother and my white apron from my cookery class. My mother was very proud of us and she gave us the money to go to the pictures the following Saturday.

Chapter Fifteen
BIRTH AND CHANGES

When my brother Harold passed his Leaving Exam, he joined the regular army. He had already spent two years in the LDF. My brother Sean was taking his Leaving Cert, and I was studying for my Inter Cert. It was 1942 and there were now eight children living at home.

But unknown to us, my mother was expecting her tenth child. Needless to say, I was oblivious of this coming event even though I was 15 years old. In those days children were not very observant, and having a baby was never mentioned, even if the person having the baby was ones own mother.

It may seem unbelievable now, but in those days we were not told the facts of life, and sex was an unmentionable word. When we entered Secondary School we were told that "we are born in a casket under our mother's heart" and I think most of us just accepted this. At one time I think I did see a movement under my mother's apron, but it went over my head, and I didn't give it another thought.

Then disaster struck our family. Just after Christmas in 1942, my mother was rushed to hospital. Although I wasn't told at the time, but heard about it later, she had had a severe haemorrhage, and needed several blood transfusions. She was very ill, and at one time was not expected to survive. On one occasion we were all taken to the hospital to see her, perhaps for the last time. She told me several years later, that seeing us all about the bed, gave her the impetus to push herself not to die, because she saw how much we needed her. She did survive but spent eight weeks in the hospital, before my youngest brother, Donal, was born was born on 26th February 1943.

While my mother was in hospital I was in charge of looking after my younger brothers and sisters. It was impossible for me to go back to school after Christmas. My mother was very ill for three months, and during those three months I was away from school. This was a crucial time for me as I was preparing to take my Inter Cert in June. But this absence had caused me to miss so much of the course, I was unable to take the exams. I did not want to have to re-do the whole year again, so I enrolled in St. Conleth's Technical School in Newbridge, and was accepted after the Easter holidays. I was to study here for the next three years.

I skipped one year and started studying in the Commercial Class. Because I had studied these subjects before and had enjoyed them, I was very happy and settled in at once.

During the war it was very difficult to get a bus from the Curragh to Newbridge, and we could not always depend on a bus arriving on time. Therefore my friend, May Brennan, and I walked to the Tech. via the Green Road and Lumville. The distance to the Tech was a little over three miles.

However, this way could prove hazardous at times, because we had to steer clear of a flock of geese that had commandeered a part of the road, and made it their own. Most mornings, cackling and hissing, they would chase us for about 50 yards. Often their beaks were inches from our legs, but we beat them every time, ending the 50 yards dash, unscathed. Perhaps in this instance, our sports training came in handy!

In the evenings on our way home from school we had the same problems. However, in winter it was more complicated because it was usually dark when we finished school, and it wasn't very pleasant walking several miles in the dark. Eventually however, things improved. We were glad the bus timetable improved, because by now, the long trek home in the evenings had lost all its attraction.

It was round about this time that my brother Harold was commissioned as a 2nd Lieutenant. It was a great day and proud day for my parents and siblings. Harold looked very handsome in his officer's uniform.

My brother Sean, together with some of his school friends, had now joined the army, and at this time was on a course in the West. In the early years of the war many people expected that Ireland might be invaded and, in a great fervour of patriotism, thousands of recruits had joined the national army. As time went on it appeared that this was not going to happen. Rumours were rife that many soldiers had deserted, and, taking the boat to England, had joined the British army.

At Mass one Sunday morning, the priest mentioned that in a particular area "a soldier came in one door and disappeared out the back door, all for *"a cup of tea and a bun."* When I returned home I asked my mother what the priest meant. Somewhat reluctantly, (it was obvious she wasn't very pleased) she explained that the priest was inferring that some of the young recruits were being bribed to desert, and join the British Army.

To assume that an Irish soldier could be bribed to desert with a cup of tea and a bun was a huge insult to the soldier but, however I did know one, he was a friend of my brothers and I am sorry to say he did not come home. There were soldiers who deserted and joined the British army, that fact is well known but it later transpired they also joined the US Army which had entered the War after Pearl Harbour. They went to fight in what they believed to be a just war.

It must be remembered that at the time of the Emergency, it was scarcely 17 years since the British had departed, and the Irish Army had taken control of the Curragh Camp. The British had occupied the Camp for almost 100 years, and there was still a good deal of pro-British sentiment around the Curragh. At the same time there were thousands of ex-British army veterans now in the Irish Army, and most of these had fought in the Great War. Many of these were bitter at the treatment they had received on joining the Irish Army, where their qualifications and experience were not recognized—though made use of—and seniority was denied them, simply because they were 'Ex-British Army.' My father was one of those.

We who were born on the Curragh were very proud, and were very fond of the buildings the British had built, and the fine roads that we cycled on, and, of course, the golf course. Returning from a visit outside the Curragh, we always looked across the plains to get our first glimpse of the majestic Watertower, with the flag flying proudly on top, flanked by the Clock Tower, and knew we would soon be home.

In our family there was always a First Communion and a Confirmation to look forward to practically every year. And of course, we, like all the children in the Curragh had our photographs taken by Donnelly Swift in his studio. Bernie and Irene made their First Communion and their Confirmation within a couple of years, round this time. The Corpus Christi Procession was another occasion when we all dressed up and carried baskets of flowers.

My brother Emmet was now in De le Salle Academy in Kildare, and I was studying for as many commercial certificates that were available in the 'Tech' I liked business methods and eventually would pursue a career in business, but now it was important for me to obtain as many academic qualifications as possible to prepare me for the future. My sister Joan would be next in line to start Secondary School in the Presentation Convent, Kildare. The rest of my siblings, with the exception of Donal, were attending the Curragh Primary School. Donal was now running round, and was being spoiled by all his sisters and brothers, and he made the most of this attention.

Now that the two eldest boys were away from home, and the younger children were growing up and becoming more independent, my mother had more time to spend with the baby Donal. It was a very happy time for the family. We missed Harold and Sean, and we always looked forward to their visits when they came home for the weekend. For me their visits invariably ended up with a visit to the Picture House. The war was on everybody's mind, and the topic of every conversation. I remember waiting to hear Radio Eireann's news bulletin at 10pm. every night. This was usually about the same time I would be trying to balance a "Trial Balance" or other homework, for the next morning at school.

Chapter Sixteen
1945

I was now 17 years old, and at an age when I was becoming more aware of what was going on in the world. Our wireless was constantly turned on from the time we woke, until the time we went to sleep. Altogether it was a hugely eventful year for the whole world—possibly the most important year of the 20th Century.

At last the war seemed to be coming to an end. At the end of April Mussolini was executed, and two days later Hitler committed suicide. On May the 5th Germany surrendered unconditionally. The war in Europe was over and on the 8th May,, VE Day was declared. The War in the Pacific continued.

One event which caused great excitement in Ireland, was the election of a new President. This took place on **25th June 1945**, and resulted in Sean T. O'Kelly being elected. I was very lucky to be nominated as a Polling Clerk in the election for the Curragh Camp. I was joined in this by a friend, Bernie Gaff. We both thoroughly enjoyed that day, and we felt very grown up. The added bonus for us was that we got paid for this work, our first real introduction to earning money!

The War in Europe was over, but in the Pacific, Japan continued to fight. Then on the 9th of August, the BBC Home Service broadcast the news that was to change the world forever. My parents had been listening to the wireless, and as usual—because we had a wireless-- many of the neighbours were crowded into our kitchen and back hall, eager to hear the latest news. The grown-ups were talking excitedly, but fearfully. I can still remember snippets of the radio announcer, *"American forces have dropped an atomic bomb on Nagasaki - the second such attack on Japan in three days" "---- is believed to have completely destroyed the city," "-----American aeroplanes warning the Japanese people that more atomic weapons would be used "again and again" to destroy the country unless they ended the war forthwith."*

Some people were crying, and some people had started to pray. People spoke about the "end of the world." It was terrifying. Visions of these astronomic explosions seemed to merge into visions of hellfire. It was very hard to sleep that night.

The whole country was shocked and horrified at what the Americans had done. It took a long time for people to accept that the Americans had really dropped such horrific weapons on 2 major cities full of civilians. Our notions of America and the American way of life, changed from that time. Needless to say 5 days after Nagasaki, Japan surrendered.

For weeks after Nagasaki most people on the Curragh were still in a state of shock. Gradually this was lifted by the prospect of the Army Tattoo. This was being held in September at the RDS in Ballsbridge, Dublin. There was a lot of movement of army trucks, tanks and dare I say it, soldiers.

For the first time in her married life, my mother and one of her friends travelled by bus to Dublin, and stayed overnight in a B&B. The following day they went to Ballsbridge to attend the Military Tattoo.. When she came back she told us that it was a great event and well worth seeing. (see photo) I think the best way to describe what it was all about is to quote from the following, author unknown. I typed this on my first day back in the 'tech' i.e. 4th September 1945:

PATRICIA O'SULLIVAN

Dermot, Irene and Bernie nursing 'Teddy' after his accident. 1942/3

The last of the ten. Left to right about 1944 Irene, Emer, Bernie and Donal. Taken near the ranges.

Mammy, Harold and Emmet on O'Connell Bridge. 1943

Mammy and friend returning from Army Tattoo 1945.

Army Tattoo 1945

End Of World War II In Europe

Brother Sean extreme right, standing 1946

Vera Melly, school friend 1946

Fellow students from Tech 1946

*Maurice Lynch, 1946
(son of Mammy's friend Mrs. Lynch)*

Fire Station Staff 1946. Father extreme left.

The Junior Section under 18 of Curragh Swimming Club. Laurie McAteer, Joan Mullan, Gertie Gaff, Joan McAteer Patty O'Sullivan and Patty McRedmond.

Blackrock Baths Co. Dublin Leinster Championships, Participants as above.

1947 Butchers Island, (sitting, sister Joan, cousin Dina Mise, cousin Sheila and two friends)

Mammy, Harold, Sean. Joan, Emer and two family friends from before the war.

Brother Sean with two friends 1947

Donnelly Swifts Sitting from left Joan, Dermot, Patty –

Standing Emmet his First Holy Communion, Harold and Sean.

PATRICIA O'SULLIVAN

Ireland needs you

Before Emergency

THE MILITARY TATOO 1945

There are many attractions in Dublin to delight the hearts of us all

And especially now in the autumn when the year is approaching its fall

But for real everlasting enjoyment I'm going to whisper to you all

That you leave not the City behind you until you have seen the Tattoo

There's a match in Croke Park on next Sunday that will not be excelled in it thrills

When Tipperary and boys from Kilenny will bring men from the towns and he hills

And after the match is all over and you're looking for something to do

Take a day from the toils of your lifetime and go out to see the Tattoo

If you're not interested in hurling and you're only a man about town

Or if you're rearing a family and the weight of your life bows you down

Take a trip to Ballsbridge in the evening, out there, there won't be queue

And you will find that you will go there more often to enjoy the Army Tattoo

There are guns, there are planes and the navy, and there are cars, trucks and bikes by the score,

There are doctors who show you you're inside, and thousands of other things more

It would take you a fortnight to see them; it's a show that is worth going to

And you are helping a Fund for the army. by attending the Army Tattoo.

author unknown'

The following academic year was going to be a serious one for me. I was entering my last year in the Tech, and it was imperative that I passed my exams at the end of the year.

We were coming to the end of the Emergency on the Curragh. One could feel the excitement of the troops as well as the families. We were aware of things happening on the Curragh. A large number of soldiers began to depart, and some families were now returning to live on the Curragh again. All Allied servicemen had been released from internment by October 1944, while all Germans servicemen had remained in the Curragh.

The State of Emergency finally lapsed on 2 September 1946. I suppose the excitement could be summed up with the following verse, author unknown. This was typed in school on the same day as its predecessor above:

JOURNEY'S END

*The day is drawing very near when we must say goodbye
To army clothes, NCOs and other larger fry,
For army grub and army stew we'll shed some salty tears
Even though it was but poorly cooked it filled us through the years,
We longed to see how we would look in a suit of Irish Green
The buttons bright that thrilled our sight and the boots with such a sheen
But now we know who made them so, and who kept the polish on
'Twill soon be just a memory when we have passed and gone*

*Our social life improved itself and we made some ribald jokes
The stuff which we had prized so much was pinched by other folk
Of girls we learnt a thing or two, we were innocents abroad
And many was the rumour that turned out to be a fraud
We learnt to smile when under fire, we grumbled now and then
But when the worst came to the worst we carried on like men
And now our days are over, our Martin Henrys are here*

*We are handing in our rifles, it does seem rather queer
We will get a one-way ticket to where we have to go
And how we will fare later, I am sure we do not know,
Some will go to the bye roads and more will do the lanes
Some will go by water and more will cross the plains
But no matter where we go we will know we have money at our back
And if we loose the job we got we will know we've got the sack.*

author unknown'

Chapter Seventeen

The End of Schooldays and Facing the Future

My examination results the previous year were very good, gave me an incentive to progress for another year. There was even talk about my going to further education at the High School of Commerce in Rathmines. Although money was scarce, my mother encouraged me to continue in the Tech for another year. This was despite the fact that I might have obtained a position in an office at this stage. Had I taken the job there would have been one less for her to worry about, particularly as the family was all getting older, and still very much dependent on the household income. But she was adamant I finish my Course.

When we returned to school in September we formed a Students' Committee. At our first meeting it was agreed that we publish a School Magazine. It was hard work, but we had a lot of encouragement from the teachers. Eventually it would be published using the old fashioned wax copying paper. A d'oly from the cookery class was used as an imprint design for the cover. Unfortunately, one of my siblings lost my copy of the magazine, but I have to say I remember it as a great success and I feel sure that my fellow students felt the same.

It was an exciting period on the Curragh at this time, particularly due to the fact that as children of the emergency, we felt that things were beginning to return to normal particularly. For us who were now teenagers, things would never be the same. We had lost most of our childhood friends, had learned to cope with very little fruit, the lack of favourite sweets etc. and being confined to a particular area of the Curragh. Of course, 'teenagers' was a word that was unheard of in most of the world. certainly in the Ireland of 1946!

We wore such awful clothes not a bit of style unless you were much older and copied designs from the films and had the money to buy the material and provided a sewing machine was part of the household furniture. I was lucky of course as my mother had a 'foot machine' a Singer. I think most of us concentrated on 'pleated' skirts and blouses, the latter were part of our 'sewing class' in the 'tech' and the finished article left a lot to be desired!

Concentrating on our studies would occupy most of our time in 1945/46. It was unheard of then to remain in school after 18 years because most of us were part of a large family and it was incumbent of us do our very best to qualify as a Junior Shorthand-Typist. However this qualification was not an open sesame to securing such a position as there were very few positions locally but we had 'prospects'

In order to show our prowess in shorthand, in 1945 our teacher suggested that we listen to Dev's reply to Churchill, which was to be broadcast on the wireless. It would be a good opportunity to show what we could do. We were to look upon this venture as 'dictation' I feel sure most people will agree that Dev was no 'Dictator' consequently my pencil spent most of the time looking skywards and not downwards, but we did our level best to 'take it all down' and I must say it nearly put me off 'shorthand' for the rest of my life. However, it did become 'child's' play as time went on and dictation became part of my life, at work of course!!!

In 1946 Nuremberg Trials took place. The Trials were closely followed in Ireland. It was very controversial at the time because the Irish Government did not recognize the legality of the trials. Being very young and impressionable at the time, and I admit, very ignorant of the facts, this had the effect of colouring my opinions. My thoughts were with the 'defeated' due to the fact that they were tried by both their 'enemies' and their 'victors.'

The 'tech' always encouraged us to apply for positions in an around Newbridge. It was looked upon as an exercise in putting our CVs together, irrespective of whether we were called for interview. We got a new B.Comm teacher round this time, and he gave us great confidence in our abilities. Academically we were all very bright, and our exam results demonstrated this. However, we were also very unsophisticated and somewhat naïve, especially in meeting new people in the grown-up world that we now had to enter.

To bolster our confidence in social activities, our new teacher introduced some very innovative lessons to the curriculum.

In our final year, in very small groups, he accompanied us to all the hotels in Newbridge. This was to give us confidence in our ability to enter the foyer of an hotel, to talk to the receptionist, and to learn how to use a phone. I think it was a great idea as it did give us a lot more confidence in our ability to conduct ourselves, in what today would be completely commonplace activities. It must be remembered that this was 1945/46.

Most eighteen year olds, especially girls of my generation had been brought up and educated in a very sheltered environment, and knew very little of the outside world. In the Convent Secondary School we had a list of rules, posted on the wall of every classroom. The first rule stated, "Immediate expulsion for company keeping of any sort," and this was lesser rules, and lesser punishment for what was considered unacceptable behaviour. In those days it was very strictly adhered to.

The Tech was coeducational and therefore somewhat different. We sometimes had ceilidhes, and the occasional dance. But very few of us had a boyfriend. The boys we met were as unsophisticated and naïve as we were. I feel sure a lot of students of that era would agree with me. But now the world was changing

I must say, however, that the production of our School Magazine gave us a great sense of achievement. The magazine, distributed to a number of businesses in the area, was received to critical acclaim. This gave a great boost to our confidence.

As it was our last year in school, it was almost obligatory for us to participate in all the school's extra-curricular activities. These included trips, social occasions, such as ceilidhes and dances, and of course, the School Camogie Team, of which I was a member. We played once a week in the sports' field, what we then called, the field behind the 'barracks' I think this is now a very famous sports' field. Our last game of camogie took us to Athy, (I think this might have been my first trip on a train). But from what I remember, we lost. In including these in school activities was another sign that times were changing—definitely for the better.

In the final year the commercial class grew in confidence, and most of my fellow students were taking our work very seriously. We were very fortunate to have a fantastic group of teachers who were determined to equip us with the best tools possible to enter the world of work. This encouraged us to do the best we could, not just for our families, and ourselves but also to show the teachers our appreciation for their efforts.

Our exams started round about May or June through the Vocational Education Committee in Naas. Like most students in their last year at school, when their exams were finished, we spent the next few months in anticipation and suspense. We returned to school in September 1946 anxiously waiting for our results.

Happily, I got the hoped for results, and I could now call myself a Junior Shorthand/Typist/Bookkeeper. My last activity in school, was to set about preparing and typing my official CV.

With the finishing of my first CV, went the hope that one day, soon perhaps, it would appear on someone's desk, and that person would find it acceptable, and I would be selected for an interview. I was filled with excitement, anticipation, and also fear at the thought that my schooldays were now over, and I was about to properly enter the adult world.

A Psalm of Life

Let us then be up and doing
With a heart for any fate;
Still achieving, still pursuing,
Learn to labour and to wait

A Psalm of Life

By Henry Wadsworth Longfellow

Ach sin sceal eile

Epilogue

When I ended the memories of my childhood it was in 1946. Sadly two years later our brother Sean, at the age of 22, died suddenly from a brain tumour. His death was a shocking blow to our parents, and it took them a long time to come to terms with his loss. At the time of his death Sean was on a course with the Ordnance Survey in the Phoenix Park (see photo taken in 1946, Sean is pictured on the extreme right, back row).

In 1955, after a long illness, our beloved mother succumbed to cancer. Our father died in 1980 at the age of 86.

When I sat down with my laptop nearly two years ago to start this memoir, there were 9 of us still alive, but sadly after a long illness, my beautiful sister Joan died in July 2009. She had had a long and happy life, although widowed at 40 she carried on with her career and never re-married She is buried with her husband Eric, a much loved brother-in-law, in her beloved Kinsale.

Life dealt us another blow a few months later when our brother, Harold died suddenly. He had served in the Army during the Emergency, and had many successes in his working life. Although 85 years old, Harold was finishing his sixth book,. He is buried in Dundalk with his children, Sean and Garry, both of whom died several years ago.

The seven remaining siblings have had long and successful careers in their chosen fields in many parts of our country. Bernie and Emer travelled the world in pursuit of their careers and are regular visitors to Ireland. My mother would have been very proud of her children, her 23 grand children and at the moment, her 20 great grand children.